MY LIFE
AND
HARD TIMES

BOOKS BY JAMES THURBER

Thurber & Company

Credos and Curios

Lanterns and Lances

The Years with Ross

Alarms and Diversions

The Wonderful O

Further Fables for Our Time

Thurber's Dogs

Thurber Country

The Thurber Album

The 13 Clocks

The Beast in Me and Other Animals

The White Deer

The Thurber Carnival

The Great Quillow

Men, Women and Dogs

Many Moons

My World—And Welcome to It

Fables for Our Time

The Last Flower

Let Your Mind Alone

The Middle-Aged Man on the Flying Trapeze

My Life and Hard Times

The Seal in the Bedroom

The Owl in the Attic

Is Sex Necessary? (with E. B. White)

PLAY

The Male Animal (with Elliott Nugent)

REVUE

The Thurber Carnival

james thurber

MY LIFE
AND
HARD TIMES

With an Introduction by John K. Hutchens
and an Afterword by Russell Baker

Commentary by Michael J. Rosen, The Thurber House

PERENNIAL ▟ CLASSICS

For
Mary A. Thurber

A hardcover edition of this book was published in 1933 by Harper & Brothers.

MY LIFE AND HARD TIMES. Copyright 1933 by James Thurber. Copyright renewed © 1961 by James Thurber. Introduction copyright © 1961 by Bantam Books, Inc. "He Knew When to Stop" copyright © 1989 by The New York Times Co. Reprinted by permission. Author biography and publication history © 1999 by Michael J. Rosen. All rights reserved. Printed in the United States of America. No part of this book may be used or reproduced in any manner whatsoever without written permission except in the case of brief quotations embodied in critical articles and reviews. For information address HarperCollins Publishers, Inc., 10 East 53rd Street, New York, NY 10022.

HarperCollins books may be purchased for educational, business, or sales promotional use. For information please write: Special Markets Department, HarperCollins Publishers, Inc., 10 East 53rd Street, New York, NY 10022.

First PERENNIAL LIBRARY edition published in 1973.

First Perennial Classics edition published 1999.
Perennial Classics are published by HarperPerennial, a division of HarperCollins Publishers.

Library of Congress Cataloging-in-Publication Data
Thurber, James, 1894–1961.
    My life and hard times / James Thurber. — 1st
Perennial Classics ed.
        p.   cm.
    ISBN 0-06-093308-9
    Includes bibliographical references.
    1. Thurber, James, 1894–1961. 2. Humorists,
American — 20th century — Biography. 3. Cartoonists —
United States — Biography. I. Title
PS3539.H94Z474   1999
818'.5209 B—dc21   99-15618

10 11 ❖/RRD 20 19

Contents

Illustrations

Introduction

The book by James Thurber that you are about to read or reread was published originally in 1933—a date which in many ways seems a lifetime ago and, indeed, in some ways *was* a lifetime ago. Think for a moment of all the gifted writers who, since then, have come and gone, and with them their books that promised to endure and did not. Then turn to *My Life and Hard Times,* and observe that it has faded not at all—that, on the contrary, it is as alive and wise and funny as it was when it was born.

This is, of course, another way of describing a classic—which is to say, a work that defies time and may even be enriched by it.

To what may be James Thurber's secret amusement, the years since he "arrived" as a distinguished writer—following his earlier success as a unique cartoonist—have found him the subject of all manner of critical interpretation. He is a humorist and a satirist. (They are not necessarily the same.) He is by nature a bitter man who escapes from melancholy by way of comedy. He is a would-be misanthrope who is innately too cheerful to be convincing in that darker role. He is a sentimentalist about animals (dogs, notably) and a realist, though usually a tolerant one, about most adult humans.

An odd, conflicting set of judgments, do you say? They would seem so, just offhand. But then, as you grow acquainted with the abundant body of work he has created, you come to realize that each of them contains some measure of truth about him. Most of these things were and still are said also of Mark Twain—which may well have been in T. S. Eliot's mind when, reviewing Thurber as an author and an artist, he saw in his work "a form of humor which is also a way of saying something serious." The man from Hannibal, Mo., and the man from Columbus, O., have much in common.

To be as many-sided as this, a writer—and we are concerned here only with Thurber as a writer—must be a literary artist both subtle and robust, which Thurber is and was from the beginning, as he demonstrated in *My Life and Hard Times,* portions of which first appeared in *The New Yorker* in the 1920s.

He gained in depth and skill as he went along, of course. A genuine writer does. In "The Secret Life of Walter Mitty" he was later to write with that acuteness of insight that makes the reader say, "This could be myself about whom I am reading." For who has not indulged in the heroics of daydreaming? It is a gift of the masters to convey the finality that Thurber achieved in that story. The name of Mitty has entered the language. His pathetic plight, and the altogether human means by which he seeks to escape it, have been drawn upon by countless other and (one trusts) grateful storytellers, along with shameless plagiarists. How many fragile, solemnly acclaimed, little-read short stories will be outlived by this one!

There were to be exercises in pure narrative craft like "The Catbird Seat," in which one could imagine a Henry James admirer (as Thurber is said to be) entertaining himself with a technically airtight plot. There were to be his fairy tales, with their grave, respectful charm and no hint of talking-down—fables like "The Wonderful O," in which a child could take delight and a grown-up could absorb a lesson about the meaning of freedom, and each could cross over into the other's province of enjoyment.

Now mere virtuosity is no great thing in a writer, and

sometimes it is a bad and diluting one. But when Thurber moves from one point to another in his remarkable range, it is with no loss of strength or style. It is, in fact, as if he found refreshment in shifting from the straight reportorial to the comic, from the piece written with love about a dog to the macabre one whose humor barely hides a nameless terror. Consider how, in *My World—And Welcome to It,* he day-dreamed with the incomparable Mitty, was bemused by the thicket of French politics, theorized hilariously about the real murderer of King Duncan in *Macbeth,* and remembered a cher-ished French poodle. That collection appeared in 1942, yet even at that fairly advanced stage in his writing life he was regarded by many as a humorist but, astonishingly, not more than that. They could not have read his nervous, nightmarish "Menaces in May," a too little-remembered story published by *The New Yorker* in 1928, or his story of a tortured, lonely man. "One Is a Wanderer," in *The Middle-Aged Man on the Flying Trapeze* (1935).

It is just possible that Thurber himself fostered this notion, for a while, of himself as a writer not to be taken seri-ously, much as did the self-deprecating Ring Lardner, with whose disenchanted comedy Thurber's darker vein has an affinity. Intent as they were on their art, the writers of the 1920s publicly cultivated a kind of off-the-cuff urbanity, and Thurber was a literary child of that decade.

But the evidence is that he matured in ratio to the serious-ness with which he did come to take himself as a writer, with what must have been his increasing awareness that he was not only a humorist in the American tradition of comic exaggera-tion but had in him the makings of a realist who would leave a cool, explicit record of life as he had seen it. The historian who wants to know in A.D. 2000 what university and newspaper life were like in an Ohio city in the second and third decades of our century cannot possibly overlook *The Thurber Album.*

Whatever the vantage point he chooses to take, and the

tone he senses is the right one for his purpose, certain common denominators are present throughout his work. He loathes cruelty. His sympathy for the out-of-luck man is as intense as his contempt for the pretentious and stupid one. He sees that children, being closer to the natural world than their elders are, have more true wisdom than adults. He finds the family life of dogs to be more rational than that of humans, and their courage and loyalty generally superior.

And there is the style that could be no one else's, a most delicate and flexible instrument, sometimes casual and chatty, and then again taut as a wire pulled tight, according to the demand made upon it. In *The Thurber Album* he tells something of what an Ohio State University professor of English, a man of classical bent, did to shape the young Thurber's mind. It was both opened and sharpened, and we can see the result today in that style in which no word is wasted, and no effect arrived at by chance.

It is not just hindsight's wisdom, I think, that recognizes how much of the mature artist is forecast in *My Life and Hard Times,* or the first twenty-odd years of James Grover Thurber, born on December 8, 1894, in Columbus. As you are about to see, it is a wonderful mingling of farce and comedy, of remembrance sometimes tender and sometimes ironic. By the time he came to write the pieces it comprises, he had served as a code clerk for the State Department in Washington and Paris, been a reporter for *The Columbus Dispatch,* the Paris edition of *The Chicago Tribune* and *The New York Evening Post,* and a contributor to and staff member of *The New Yorker.* In the sense approved by his 1920s generation, he had been around. But as he goes back in time to his starting point, the voice remains Middle Western as surely as his accent does to this day. He is neither the debonair expatriate making fun of his native heath nor the sentimental alumnus returning to the old campus.

As these prefatory notes on him have suggested, Thurber went on from there to do more complex work, but none finer

of its kind, none more precisely successful in terms of its inten-
tion, than this memoir of his boyhood and young manhood.
"Humor is emotional chaos remembered in tranquility," he
once said, neatly rephrasing Wordsworth on poetry. How
delightful is the chaos here, and how inspired is the remember-
ing. "The Night the Bed Fell" and "The Day the Dam Broke"
and "The Night the Ghost Got In" are waiting to tell you—
these and others of the ten items in *My Life and Hard Times*.
Some of them are in a vein of farce more emphatic than he has
since used. But even the wild scramble of "The Day the Dam
Broke," you will note, has a subtly effective tactic typical of the
later Thurber—i.e., the dam did *not* break, and the citizenry's
rush to safe ground was unnecessary. As early as that, in the
Thurber world, people behaved rather more foolishly than a
self-respecting dog would do.

Everyone will have his favorites among these Thurberian
memories. My own would have to include "The Dog That Bit
People," if only for what it says of the narrator's mother. What
woman except Mrs. Thurber would have praised a dog that
impaired the family's finances by biting an important business
associate of her husband?—the dog being clearly right, she
said, because he was a student of character who recognized the
victim as untrustworthy. In Thurber's Columbus the off-beat
consistently has its own superb logic. In that Thurber household even the mice behaved oddly, and Grandfather, a Civil
War veteran, proved difficult only when his mind did *not*
remain fixed in the past.

"It is one of the few things in my life I would like to live
over again if I could. I don't suppose that I can, now," the
author observes at one point. He is speaking of a particular
incident, but one must believe that he is thinking of that whole,
long-gone time. Something was always happening. The damp
hand of melancholy of which he writes in his 1933 preface to
My Life and Hard Times had not yet settled upon a generation
and the world.

"An autobiography? A memoir?" literal-minded doubters exclaim when Thurber adherents refer to this book as being more or less specifically the truth. "Who could remember all this so exactly, including conversations held twenty years and more before?"

"Have a care," the adherents answer, "because it is likely that few men living possess so nearly the power of total recall as this one does." It was true even then, when he was a youngster, and long before he was borne in upon himself by progressing blindness. As a psychology student at Ohio State he scored 78 percent when asked to write down what he could remember of a 1,000-word article read to his class. No one in his group was close to him. And this is important, because it means that the author of *My Life and Hard Times* had no need whatever to resort to those nostalgic fictions that infest a whole literature of childhood reminiscence. Simply and firmly, he went home. Apart from the artist's license to foreshorten time and alter the order of incident, I, for one, wouldn't care to challenge the most minute detail of what Thurber represents to be the truth. In sum, of course, it *is* the truth, in the sense that matters.

All this has something to do with the fact that now, in his almost complete blindness, he is an even finer writer than he has ever been. A man less gallant, less passionately dedicated to the exactly used word, might have been crushed by the personal tragedy that overcame him. Thurber actually turned it to his advantage.

"A blind man benefits by lack of distinctions," he said recently, not long after he had declared that "my one-eighth vision happily obscures sad and ungainly sights, leaving only the vivid and the radiant, some of whom are my friends and neighbors." If this meant that he could no longer draw as he once did, it also meant an even sharper concentration on the art that remained to him. The figures bear this out. The last fifteen years have been his most productive ones as a writer.

He has gone afield for reportorial pieces for *The New Yorker,* into his imagination for those fantasies ostensibly for children but actually for all of us, and into his memory and the records for his remarkable biography of the late Harold Ross, editor of *The New Yorker,* his friend and greatly valued mentor.

Another friend, Lewis Gannett, the critic, has reported that in that inner world of the blind and in the silence of the night Thurber tastes and shapes the words he will be dictating the next day, arranging and rearranging cadences, editing and discarding. When they are read back to him he edits yet again, sometimes repeating the whole process ten times. It is small wonder that the later prose of a man who always has been a precisionist in language is distilled to something like perfection, while retaining that apparently easy spontaneity of his early and middle phases. With *The Male Animal,* the Broadway comedy hit that he wrote with Elliott Nugent in 1940, what might long have been assumed became entirely obvious: that he wrote for the ear as surely as he drew for the eye. Now, hearing every word in his mind before he speaks it, and then hearing it again when he does speak it, he has inevitably refined his art still further.

That this art was true from the very beginning, the pages that follow attest beyond any doubt. What it comes to, in sum, is that we have here a writer original, versatile, and, except in quality, unpredictable. A new generation having come along since *My Life and Hard Times* made its opening bow, some will now be meeting him for the first time. They are to be envied.

—John K. Hutchens

Preface to a Life

❦

Benvenuto Cellini said that a man should be at least forty years old before he undertakes so fine an enterprise as that of setting down the story of his life. He said also that an autobiographer should have accomplished something of excellence. Nowadays nobody who has a typewriter pays any attention to the old master's quaint rules. I myself have accomplished nothing of excellence except a remarkable and, to some of my friends, unaccountable expertness in hitting empty ginger ale bottles with small rocks at a distance of thirty paces. Moreover, I am not yet forty years old. But the grim date moves toward me apace; my legs are beginning to go, things blur before my eyes, and the faces of the rose-lipped maids I knew in my twenties are misty as dreams.

At forty my faculties may have closed up like flowers at evening, leaving me unable to write my memoirs with a fitting and discreet inaccuracy or, having written them, unable to carry them to the publisher's. A writer verging into the middle years lives in dread of losing his way to the publishing house and wandering down to the Bowery or the Battery, there to disappear like Ambrose Bierce. He has sometimes also the kindred dread of turning a sudden corner and meeting himself sauntering along in the opposite direction. I have known writers at this dangerous and tricky age to phone their homes from their offices, or their offices from their homes, ask for themselves in a low tone, and then, having fortunately discovered that they were "out," to collapse in hard-breathing relief. This is particularly true of writers of light pieces running from a thousand to two thousand words.

The notion that such persons are gay of heart and carefree is curiously untrue. They lead, as a matter of fact, an existence of jumpiness and apprehension. They sit on the edge of the chair of Literature. In the house of Life they have the feeling that they have never taken off their overcoats. Afraid of losing themselves in the larger flight of the two-volume novel, or even the one-volume novel, they stick to short accounts of their misadventures because they never get so deep into them but that they feel they can get out. This type of writing is not a joyous form of self-expression but the manifestation of a twitchiness at once cosmic and mundane. Authors of such pieces have, nobody knows why, a genius for getting into minor difficulties: they walk into the wrong apartments, they drink furniture polish for stomach bitters, they drive their cars into the prize tulip beds of haughty neighbors, they playfully slap gangsters, mistaking them for old school friends. To call such persons "humorists," a loose-fitting and ugly word, is to miss the nature of their dilemma and the dilemma of their nature. The little wheels of their invention are set in motion by the damp hand of melancholy.

Such a writer moves about restlessly wherever he goes, ready to get the hell out at the drop of a pie-pan or the lift of a skirt. His gestures are the ludicrous reflexes of the maladjusted; his repose is the momentary inertia of the nonplussed. He pulls the blinds against the morning and creeps into smoky corners at night. He talks largely about small matters and smally about great affairs. His ears are shut to the ominous rumblings of the dynasties of the world moving toward a cloudier chaos than ever before, but he hears with an acute perception the startling sounds that rabbits make twisting in the bushes along a country road at night and a cold chill comes upon him when the comic supplement of a Sunday newspaper blows unexpectedly out of an areaway and envelopes his knees. He can sleep while the commonwealth crumbles but a strange sound in the pantry at three in the morning will strike terror into his stomach. He is not afraid, or much aware, of the menaces of empire but he keeps looking behind him as he walks along darkening streets out of the fear that he is being softly followed by little men padding along in single file, about a foot and a half high, large-eyed, and whiskered.

It is difficult for such a person to conform to what Ford Madox Ford in his book of recollections has called the sole reason for writing one's memoirs: namely, to paint a picture of one's time. Your shortpiece writer's time is not Walter Lippmann's time, or Stuart Chase's time, or Professor Einstein's time. It is his own personal time, circumscribed by the short boundaries of his pain and his embarrassment, in which what happens to his digestion, the rear axle of his car, and the confused flow of his relationships with six or eight persons and two or three buildings is of greater importance than what goes on in the nation or in the universe. He knows vaguely that the nation is not much good any more; he has read that the crust of the earth is shrinking alarmingly and that the universe is growing steadily colder, but he does not believe that any of the three is in half as bad shape as he is.

Enormous strides are made in star-measurement, theoretical economics, and the manufacture of bombing planes, but he usually doesn't find out about them until he picks up an old copy of "Time" on a picnic grounds or in the summer house of a friend. He is aware that billions of dollars are stolen every year by bankers and politicians, and that thousands of people are out of work, but these conditions do not worry him a tenth as much as the conviction that he has wasted three months on a stupid psychoanalyst or the suspicion that a piece he has been working on for two long days was done much better and probably more quickly by Robert Benchley in 1924.

The "time" of such a writer, then, is hardly worth reading

about if the reader wishes to find out what was going on in the world while the writer in question was alive and at what might be laughingly called "his best." All that the reader is going to find out is what happened to the writer. The compensation, I suppose, must lie in the comforting feeling that one has had, after all, a pretty sensible and peaceful life, by comparison. It is unfortunate, however, that even a well-ordered life can not lead anybody safely around the inevitable doom that waits in the skies. As F. Hopkinson Smith long ago pointed out, the claw of the sea-puss gets us all in the end.

J. T.

Sandy Hook,
Connecticut,
September 25, 1933

MY LIFE
AND
HARD TIMES

1

❦

The Night the Bed Fell

I suppose that the high-water mark of my youth in Columbus, Ohio, was the night the bed fell on my father. It makes a better recitation (unless, as some friends of mine have said, one has heard it five or six times) than it does a piece of writing, for it is almost necessary to throw furniture around, shake doors, and bark like a dog, to lend the proper atmosphere and verisimilitude to what is admittedly a somewhat incredible tale. Still, it did take place.

It happened, then, that my father had decided to sleep in the attic one night, to be away where he could think. My mother opposed the notion strongly because, she said, the old wooden bed up there was unsafe: it was wobbly and the heavy headboard would crash down on father's head in case the bed fell, and kill him. There was no dissuading him, however, and at a quarter past ten he closed the attic door behind him and went up the narrow twisting stairs. We later heard ominous creakings as he crawled into bed. Grandfather, who usually slept in the attic bed when he was with us, had disappeared some days before. (On these occasions he was usually gone six or eight days and returned growling and out of temper, with the news that the federal Union was run by a passel of blockheads and that the Army of the Potomac didn't have any more chance than a fiddler's bitch.)

We had visiting us at this time a nervous first cousin of mine named Briggs Beall, who believed that he was likely to cease breathing when he was asleep. It was his feeling that if he were not awakened every hour during the night, he might die of suffocation. He had been accustomed to setting an alarm clock to ring at intervals until morning, but I persuaded him to abandon this. He slept in my room and I told him that I was such a light sleeper that if anybody quit breathing in the same room with me, I would wake instantly. He tested me the first night—which I had suspected he would—by holding his breath after my regular breathing had convinced him I was asleep. I was not asleep, however, and called to him. This seemed to allay his fears a little, but he took the precaution of putting a glass of spirits of camphor on a little table at the head of his bed. In case I didn't arouse him until he was almost gone, he said, he would sniff the camphor, a powerful reviver. Briggs was not the only member of his family who had his crotchets. Old Aunt Melissa Beall (who could whistle like a man, with two fingers in her mouth) suffered under the premonition that she was destined to die on South High Street, because she had been born on South High Street and married on South High Street. Then there was Aunt Sarah Shoaf, who never went to bed at night without the fear that a burglar was going to get in and blow chloroform under her door through a tube. To avert this calamity—for she was in greater dread of anesthetics than of losing her household goods—she always piled her money, silverware, and other valuables in a neat stack just outside her bedroom, with a note reading: "This is all I have. Please take it and do not use your chloroform, as this is all I have." Aunt Grace Shoaf also had a burglar phobia, but she met it with more fortitude. She was confident that burglars had been getting into her house every night for forty years. The fact that she never missed anything was to her no proof to the contrary. She always claimed that she scared them off before they could take anything, by throwing shoes down the hallway. When she went to bed she piled, where she could get at them handily, all the shoes there were about her house. Five minutes after she had turned off the light, she would sit up in bed and say "Hark!" Her husband, who had learned to ignore the whole situation as long ago as 1903, would either be sound asleep or pretend to be sound asleep. In either case he would not respond to her tugging and pulling, so that presently she would arise, tiptoe to the door, open it slightly and heave a shoe down the hall in one direction, and its mate down the hall in the other direction. Some nights she threw them all, some nights only a couple of pair.

But I am straying from the remarkable incidents that took place during the night that the bed fell on father. By midnight we were all in bed. The layout of the rooms and the disposition of their occupants is important to an understanding of what later occurred. In the front room upstairs (just under father's attic bedroom) were my mother and my brother Herman, who sometimes sang in his sleep, usually "Marching Through Georgia" or "Onward, Christian Soldiers." Briggs Beall and myself were in a room adjoining this one. My brother Roy was in a room across the hall from ours. Our bull terrier, Rex, slept in the hall.

My bed was an army cot, one of those affairs which are made wide enough to sleep on comfortably only by putting up, flat with the middle section, the two sides which ordinarily hang down like the sideboards of a drop-leaf table. When these sides are up, it is perilous to roll too far toward the edge, for then the cot is likely to tip completely over, bringing the whole bed down on top of one, with a tremendous banging crash. This, in fact, is precisely what happened, about two o'clock in the morning. (It was my mother who, in recalling the scene later, first referred to it as "the night the bed fell on your father.")

Some nights she threw them all.

Always a deep sleeper, slow to arouse (I had lied to Briggs), I was at first unconscious of what had happened when the iron cot rolled me onto the floor and toppled over on me. It left me still warmly bundled up and unhurt, for the bed rested above me like a canopy. Hence I did not wake up, only reached the edge of consciousness and went back. The racket, however, instantly awakened my mother, in the next room, who came to the immediate conclusion that her worst dread was realized: the big wooden bed upstairs had fallen on father. She therefore screamed, "Let's go to your poor father!" It was this shout, rather than the noise of my cot falling, that awakened Herman, in the same room with her. He thought that mother had become, for no apparent reason, hysterical. "You're all right, Mamma!" he shouted, trying to calm her. They exchanged shout for shout for perhaps ten seconds: "Let's go to your poor father!" and "You're all right!" That

He came to the conclusion that he was suffocating.

woke up Briggs. By this time I was conscious of what was going on, in a vague way, but did not yet realize that I was under my bed instead of on it. Briggs, awakening in the midst of loud shouts of fear and apprehension, came to the quick conclusion that he was suffocating and that we were all trying to "bring him out." With a low moan, he grasped the glass of camphor at the head of his bed and instead of sniffing it poured it over himself. The room reeked of camphor. "Ugf, ahfg," choked Briggs, like a drowning man, for he had almost succeeded in stopping his breath under the deluge of pungent spirits. He leaped out of bed and groped toward the open window, but he came up against one that was closed. With his hand, he beat out the glass, and I could hear it crash and tinkle on the alleyway below. It was at this juncture that I, in trying to get up, had the uncanny sensation of feeling my bed above me! Foggy with sleep, I now suspected, in my turn, that the whole uproar was being made in a frantic endeavor to extricate me from what must be an unheard-of and perilous situation. "Get me out of this!" I bawled. "Get me out!" I think I had the nightmarish belief that I was entombed in a mine. "Gugh," gasped Briggs, floundering in his camphor.

By this time my mother, still shouting, pursued by Herman, still shouting, was trying to open the door to the attic, in order to go up and get my father's body out of the wreckage. The door was stuck, however, and wouldn't yield. Her frantic pulls on it only added to the general banging and confusion. Roy and the dog were now up, the one shouting questions, the other barking.

Father, farthest away and soundest sleeper of all, had by this time been awakened by the battering on the attic door. He decided that the house was on fire. "I'm coming, I'm coming!" he wailed in a slow, sleepy voice—it took him many minutes to regain full consciousness. My mother, still believing he was caught under the bed, detected in his "I'm coming!" the

Roy had to throw Rex.

mournful, resigned note of one who is preparing to meet his Maker. "He's dying!" she shouted.

"I'm all right!" Briggs yelled to reassure her. "I'm all right!" He still believed that it was his own closeness to death that was worrying mother. I found at last the light switch in my room, unlocked the door, and Briggs and I joined the others at the attic door. The dog, who never did like Briggs, jumped for him—assuming that he was the culprit in whatever was going on—and Roy had to throw Rex and hold him. We could hear father crawling out of bed upstairs. Roy pulled the attic door open, with a mighty jerk, and father came down the stairs, sleepy and irritable but safe and sound. My mother began to weep when she saw him. Rex began to howl. "What in the name of God is going on here?" asked father.

The situation was finally put together like a gigantic jigsaw puzzle. Father caught a cold from prowling around in his bare feet but there were no other bad results. "I'm glad," said mother, who always looked on the bright side of things, "that your grandfather wasn't here."

2

The Car We Had to Push

Many autobiographers, among them Lincoln Steffens and Ger-
trude Atherton, describe earthquakes their families have been
in. I am unable to do this because my family was never in
an earthquake, but we went through a number of things in
Columbus that were a great deal like earthquakes. I remember
in particular some of the repercussions of an old Reo we had
that wouldn't go unless you pushed it for quite a way and suddenly let your clutch out. Once, we had been able to start the
engine easily by cranking it, but we had had the car for so
many years that finally it wouldn't go unless you pushed it and
let your clutch out. Of course, it took more than one person to
do this; it took sometimes as many as five or six, depending on
the grade of the roadway and conditions underfoot. The car
was unusual in that the clutch and brake were on the same
pedal, making it quite easy to stall the engine after it got
started, so that the car would have to be pushed again.

My father used to get sick at his stomach pushing the car,
and very often was unable to go to work. He had never liked
the machine, even when it was good, sharing my ignorance
and suspicion of all automobiles of twenty years ago and
longer. The boys I went to school with used to be able to

It took sometimes as many as five or six.

identify every car as it passed by: Thomas Flyer, Firestone-Columbus, Stevens Duryea, Rambler, Winton, White Steamer, etc. I never could. The only car I was really interested in was one that the Get-Ready Man, as we called him, rode around town in: a big Red Devil with a door in the back. The Get-Ready Man was a lank unkempt elderly gentleman with wild eyes and a deep voice who used to go about shouting at people through a megaphone to prepare for the end of the world. "Get ready! Get read-y!" he would bellow. "The Worllld is coming to an End!" His startling exhortations would come up, like summer thunder, at the most unexpected times and in the most surprising places. I remember once during Mantell's production of "King Lear" at the Colonial Theatre, that the Get-Ready Man added his bawlings to the squealing of Edgar and the ranting of the King and the mouthing of the Fool, rising from somewhere in the balcony to join in. The theatre was in absolute darkness and there were rumblings of thunder and flashes of lightning offstage. Neither father nor I, who were there, ever completely got over the scene, which went something like this:

Edgar: Tom's a-cold.—O, do de, do de, do de!—Bless thee from whirlwinds, star-blasting, and taking . . . the foul fiend vexes!

(Thunder off.)

Lear: What! Have his daughters brought him to this pass?—

Get-Ready Man: Get ready! Get ready!

Edgar: Pillicock sat on Pillicock-hill:—

Halloo, halloo, loo, loo!
(Lightning flashes.)

Get-Ready Man: The Worllld is com-ing to an End!

Fool: This cold night will turn us all to fools and madmen!

Edgar: Take heed o' the foul fiend: obey thy paren——

Get-Ready Man: Get *Rea*-dy!

Edgar: Tom's a-*cold!*

Get-Ready Man: The *Worr*-uld is coming to an end! . . .

They found him finally, and ejected him, still shouting. The Theatre, in our time, has known few such moments.

But to get back to the automobile. One of my happiest memories of it was when, in its eighth year, my brother Roy got together a great many articles from the kitchen, placed them in a square of canvas, and swung this under the car with a string attached to it so that, at a twitch, the canvas would give way and the steel and tin things would clatter to the street. This was a little scheme of Roy's to frighten father, who had always expected the car might explode. It worked perfectly. That was twenty-five years ago, but it is one of the few things in my life I would like to live over again if I could. I don't suppose that I can, now. Roy twitched the string in the middle of a lovely afternoon, on Bryden Road near Eighteenth Street. Father had closed his eyes and, with his hat off, was enjoying a cool breeze. The clatter on the asphalt was tremendously effective: knives, forks, can-openers, pie pans, pot lids, biscuit-cutters, ladles, egg-beaters fell, beautifully together, in a lingering, clamant crash. "Stop the *car!*" shouted father. "I can't," Roy said. "The engine fell out." "God Almighty!" said father, who knew what *that* meant, or knew what it sounded as if it might mean.

It ended unhappily, of course, because we finally had to drive back and pick up the stuff and even father knew the difference between the works of an automobile and the equipment of a pantry. My mother wouldn't have known, however, nor *her* mother. My mother, for instance, thought—or, rather, knew—that it was dangerous to drive an automobile without gasoline: it fried the valves, or something. "Now don't you dare drive all over town without gasoline!" she would say to us when we started off. Gasoline, oil, and water were much the

The Get-Ready Man.

same to her, a fact that made her life both confusing and perilous. Her greatest dread, however, was the Victrola—we had a very early one, back in the "Come Josephine in My Flying Machine" days. She had an idea that the Victrola might blow up. It alarmed her, rather than reassured her, to explain that the photograph was run neither by gasoline nor by electricity. She could only suppose that it was propelled by some newfangled and untested apparatus which was likely to let go at any minute, making us all the victims and martyrs of the wild-eyed Edison's dangerous experiments. The telephone she was comparatively at peace with, except, of course, during storms, when for some reason or other she always took the receiver off the hook and let it hang. She came naturally by her confused and groundless fears, for her own mother lived the latter years of her life in the horrible suspicion that electricity was dripping invisibly all over the house. It leaked, she contended, out of empty sockets if the wall switch had been left on. She would go around screwing in bulbs, and if they lighted up she would hastily and fearfully turn off the wall switch and go back to her *Pearson's* or *Everybody's,* happy in the satisfaction that she had stopped not only a costly but a dangerous leakage. Nothing could ever clear this up for her.

Our poor old Reo came to a horrible end, finally. We had parked it too far from the curb on a street with a car line. It was late at night and the street was dark. The first streetcar that came along couldn't get by. It picked up the tired old automobile as a terrier might seize a rabbit and drubbed it unmercifully, losing its hold now and then but catching a new grip a second later. Tires booped and whooshed, the fenders queeled and graked, the steering-wheel rose up like a spectre and disappeared in the direction of Franklin Avenue with a melancholy whistling sound, bolts and gadgets flew like sparks from a Catherine wheel. It was a splendid spectacle but, of course, saddening to everybody (except the motorman of the streetcar, who was sore). I think some of us broke down and wept. It

Electricity was leaking all over the house.

must have been the weeping that caused grandfather to take on so terribly. Time was all mixed up in his mind; automobiles and the like he never remembered having seen. He apparently gathered, from the talk and excitement and weeping, that somebody had died. Nor did he let go of this delusion. He insisted, in fact, after almost a week in which we strove mightily to divert him, that it was a sin and a shame and a disgrace on the family to put the funeral off any longer. "Nobody is dead! The automobile is smashed!" shouted my father, trying for the thirtieth time to explain the situation to the old man. "Was he drunk?" demanded grandfather, sternly. "Was who drunk?" asked father. "Zenas," said grandfather. He had a name for the corpse now: it was his brother Zenas, who, as it happened, *was* dead, but not from driving an automobile while intoxicated. Zenas had died in 1866. A sensitive, rather poetical boy of twenty-one when the Civil War broke out, Zenas had gone to South America—"just," as he wrote back, "until it blows over." Returning after the war had blown over, he caught the same disease that was killing off the chestnut trees in those years, and passed away. It was the only case in history where a tree doctor had to be called in to spray a person, and our family had felt it very keenly; nobody else in the United States caught the blight. Some of us have looked upon Zenas' fate as a kind of poetic justice.

Now that grandfather knew, so to speak, who was dead, it became increasingly awkward to go on living in the same house with him as if nothing had happened. He would go into towering rages in which he threatened to write to the Board of Health unless the funeral were held at once. We realized that something had to be done. Eventually, we persuaded a friend of father's, named George Martin, to dress up in the manner and costume of the eighteen-sixties and pretend to be Uncle Zenas, in order to set grandfather's mind at rest. The impostor looked fine and impressive in sideburns and a high beaver hat, and not unlike the daguerreotypes of Zenas in our album. I

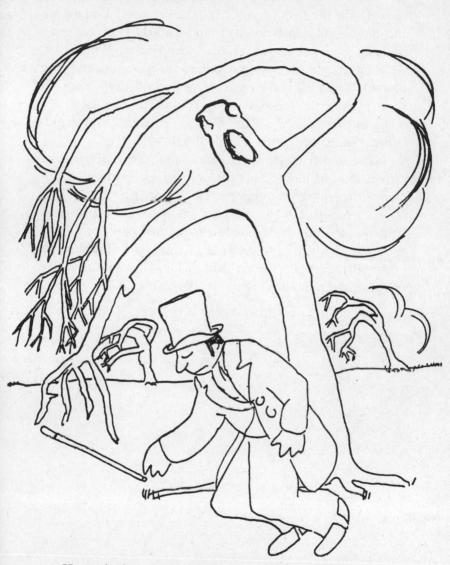

He caught the same disease that was killing the chestnut trees.

shall never forget the night, just after dinner, when this Zenas walked into the living-room. Grandfather was stomping up and down, tall, hawk-nosed, round-oathed. The newcomer held out both his hands. "Clem!" he cried to grandfather. Grandfather turned slowly, looked at the intruder, and snorted. "Who air *you*?" he demanded in his deep, resonant voice. "I'm Zenas!" cried Martin. "Your brother Zenas, fit as a fiddle and sound as a dollar!" "Zenas, my foot!" said grandfather. "Zenas died of the chestnut blight in '66!"

Grandfather was given to these sudden, unexpected, and extremely lucid moments; they were generally more embarrassing than his other moments. He comprehended before he went to bed that night that the old automobile had been destroyed and that its destruction had caused all the turmoil in the house. "It flew all to pieces, Pa," my mother told him, in graphically describing the accident. "I knew 'twould," growled grandfather. "I allus told ye to git a Pope-Toledo."

3

The Day the Dam Broke

My memories of what my family and I went through during the 1913 flood in Ohio I would gladly forget. And yet neither the hardships we endured nor the turmoil and confusion we experienced can alter my feeling toward my native state and city. I am having a fine time now and wish Columbus were here, but if anyone ever wished a city was in hell it was during that frightful and perilous afternoon in 1913 when the dam broke, or, to be more exact, when everybody in town *thought* that the dam broke. We were both ennobled and demoralized by the experience. Grandfather especially rose to magnificent heights which can never lose their splendor for me, even though his reactions to the flood were based upon a profound misconception; namely, that Nathan Bedford Forrest's cavalry was the menace we were called upon to face. The only possible means of escape for us was to flee the house, a step which grandfather sternly forbade, brandishing his old army sabre in his hand. "Let the sons —— come!" he roared. Meanwhile hundreds of people were streaming by our house in wild panic, screaming "Go east! Go east!" We had to stun grandfather with the ironing board. Impeded as we were by the inert form of the old gentleman—he was taller than six feet and weighed almost a hundred and seventy pounds—we were passed, in the first half-mile, by practically everybody else in the city. Had grandfather not come to, at the corner of Parsons Avenue and Town Street, we would unquestionably have been overtaken and engulfed by the roaring waters—that is, if there had *been* any roaring waters. Later, when the panic had died down and people had gone rather sheepishly back to their homes and their offices, minimizing the distances they had run and offering various reasons for running, city engineers pointed out that even if the dam had broken, the water level would not have risen more than two additional inches in the West Side. The West Side was, at the time of the dam scare, under thirty feet of water—as, indeed, were all Ohio river towns during the great spring floods of twenty years ago. The East Side (where we lived and where all the running occurred) had never been in any danger at all. Only a rise of some ninety-five feet could have caused the flood waters to flow over High Street—the thoroughfare that divided the east side of town from the west—and engulf the East Side.

The fact that we were all as safe as kittens under a cookstove did not, however, assuage in the least the fine despair and the grotesque desperation which seized upon the residents of the East Side when the cry spread like a grass fire that the dam had given way. Some of the most dignified, staid, cynical, and clear-thinking men in town abandoned their wives, stenographers, homes, and offices and ran east. There are few alarms in the world more terrifying than "The dam has broken!" There are few persons capable of stopping to reason when that clarion cry strikes upon their ears, even persons who live in towns no nearer than five hundred miles to a dam.

The Columbus, Ohio, broken-dam rumor began, as I recall it, about noon of March 12, 1913. High Street, the main canyon of trade, was loud with the placid hum of business and the buzzing of placid businessmen arguing, computing, wheedling, offering, refusing, compromising. Darius Conningway, one of the foremost corporation lawyers in the Middle-West, was telling the Public Utilities Commission in the language of Julius Caesar that they might as well try to move the Northern star as to move him. Other men were making their little boasts and their little gestures. Suddenly somebody began to run. It may be that he had simply remembered, all of a moment, an engagement to meet his wife, for which he was now frightfully late. Whatever it was, he ran east on Broad Street (probably toward the Maramor Restaurant, a favorite place for a man to meet his wife). Somebody else began to run, perhaps a newsboy in high spirits. Another man, a portly gentleman of affairs, broke into a trot. Inside of ten minutes, everybody on High Street, from the Union Depot to the Courthouse was running. A loud mumble gradually crystallized into the dread word "dam." "The dam has broke!" The fear was put into words by a little old lady in an electric, or by a traffic cop, or by a small boy: nobody knows who, nor does it now really matter. Two thousand people were abruptly in full flight. "Go east!" was the cry that arose—east away from the river, east to safety. "Go east! Go east! Go east!"

Black streams of people flowed eastward down all the streets leading in that direction; these streams, whose headwaters were in the dry goods stores, office buildings, harness shops, movie theatres, were fed by trickles of housewives, children, cripples, servants, dogs, and cats, slipping out of the houses past which the main streams flowed, shouting and screaming. People ran out leaving fires burning and food cooking and doors wide open. I remember, however, that my mother turned out all the fires and that she took with her a dozen eggs and two loaves of bread. It was her plan to make Memorial Hall, just two blocks away, and take refuge somewhere in the top of it, in one of the dusty rooms where war veterans met and where old battleflags and stage scenery were stored. But the seething throngs, shouting "Go east!," drew her along and the rest of us with her. When grandfather

Two thousand people were in full flight.

regained full consciousness, at Parsons Avenue, he turned upon the retreating mob like a vengeful prophet and exhorted the men to form ranks and stand off the Rebel dogs, but at length he, too, got the idea that the dam had broken and, roaring "Go east!" in his powerful voice, he caught up in one arm a small child and in the other a slight clerkish man of perhaps forty-two and we slowly began to gain on those ahead of us.

A scattering of firemen, policemen, and army officers in dress uniforms—there had been a review at Fort Hayes, in the northern part of town—added color to the surging billows of people. "Go east!" cried a little child in a piping voice, as she ran past a porch on which drowsed a lieutenant-colonel of infantry. Used to quick decisions, trained to immediate obedience, the officer bounded off the porch and, running at full tilt, soon passed the child, bawling "Go east!" The two of them emptied rapidly the houses of the little street they were on. "What is it? What is it?" demanded a fat, waddling man who intercepted the colonel. The officer dropped behind and asked the little child what it was. "The dam has broke!" gasped the girl. "The dam has broke!" roared the colonel. "Go east! Go east! Go east!" He was soon leading, with the exhausted child in his arms, a fleeing company of three hundred persons who had gathered around him from living-rooms, shops, garages, backyards, and basements.

Nobody has ever been able to compute with any exactness how many people took part in the great rout of 1913, for the panic, which extended from the Winslow Bottling Works in the South End to Clintonville, six miles north, ended as abruptly as it began and the bobtail and ragtag and velvet-gowned groups of refugees melted away and slunk home, leaving the streets peaceful and deserted. The shouting, weeping, tangled evacuation of the city lasted not more than two hours in all. Some few people got as far east as Reynoldsburg, twelve miles away; fifty or more reached the Country Club, eight miles away; most of the others gave up, exhausted, or climbed trees in Franklin Park, four miles out. Order was restored and fear dispelled finally by means of militiamen riding about in motor lorries bawling through megaphones: "The dam has *not* broken!" At first this tended only to add to the confusion and increase the panic, for many stampeders thought the soldiers were bellowing "The dam has now broken!," thus setting an official seal of authentication on the calamity.

All the time, the sun shone quietly and there was nowhere any sign of oncoming waters. A visitor in an airplane, looking down on the straggling, agitated masses of people below, would have been hard put to it to divine a reason for the phenomenon. It must have inspired, in such an observer, a peculiar kind of terror, like the sight of the *Marie Celeste,* abandoned at sea, its galley fires peacefully burning, its tranquil decks bright in the sunlight.

An aunt of mine, Aunt Edith Taylor, was in a movie theatre on High Street when, over and above the sound of the piano in the pit (a W. S. Hart picture was being shown), there rose the steadily increasing tromp of running feet. Persistent shouts rose above the tromping. An elderly man, sitting near my aunt, mumbled something, got out of his seat, and went up the aisle at a dogtrot. This started everybody. In an instant the audience was jamming the aisles. "Fire!" shouted a woman who always expected to be burned up in a theatre; but now the shouts outside were louder and coherent: "The dam has broke!" cried somebody. "Go east!" screamed a small woman in front of my aunt. And east they went, pushing and shoving and clawing, knocking women and children down, emerging finally into the street, torn and sprawling. Inside the theatre, Bill Hart was calmly calling some desperado's bluff and the brave girl at the piano played "Row! Row! Row!" loudly and then "In My Harem." Outside, men were streaming across the Statehouse yard, others were climbing trees, a woman managed to get up onto the "These Are My Jewels" statue, whose bronze figures of Sherman, Stanton, Grant, and Sheridan

One woman climbed up onto the "These Are My Jewels" statue.

watched with cold unconcern the going to pieces of the capital city.

"I ran south to State Street, east on State to Third, south on Third to Town, and out east on Town," my Aunt Edith has written me. "A tall spare woman with grim eyes and a determined chin ran past me down the middle of the street. I was still uncertain as to what was the matter, in spite of all the shouting. I drew up alongside the woman with some effort, for although she was in her fifties, she had a beautiful easy running form and seemed to be in excellent condition. 'What is it?' I puffed. She gave me a quick glance and then looked ahead again, stepping up her pace a trifle. 'Don't ask me, ask God!' she said.

"When I reached Grant Avenue, I was so spent that Dr. H. R. Mallory—you remember Dr. Mallory, the man with the white beard who looks like Robert Browning?—well, Dr. Mallory, whom I had drawn away from at the corner of Fifth and Town, passed me. 'It's got us!' he shouted, and I felt sure that whatever it was *did* have us, for you know what conviction Dr. Mallory's statements always carried. I didn't know at that time what he meant, but I found out later. There was a boy behind him on roller-skates, and Dr. Mallory mistook the swishing of the skates for the sound of rushing water. He eventually reached the Columbus School for Girls, at the corner of Parsons Avenue and Town Street, where he collapsed, expecting the cold frothing waters of the Scioto to sweep him into oblivion. The boy on the skates swirled past him and Dr. Mallory realized for the first time what he had been running from. Looking back up the street, he could see no signs of water, but nevertheless, after resting a few minutes, he jogged on east again. He caught up with me at Ohio Avenue, where we rested together. I should say that about seven hundred people passed us. A funny thing was that all of them were on foot. Nobody seemed to have had the courage to stop and start his car; but as

"It's got us!" he shouted.

I remember it, all cars had to be cranked in those days, which is probably the reason."

The next day, the city went about its business as if nothing had happened, but there was no joking. It was two years or more before you dared treat the breaking of the dam lightly. And even now, twenty years after, there are a few persons, like Dr. Mallory, who will shut up like a clam if you mention the Afternoon of the Great Run.

4

The Night the Ghost Got In

The ghost that got into our house on the night of November 17, 1915, raised such a hullabaloo of misunderstanding that I am sorry I didn't just let it keep on walking, and go to bed. Its advent caused my mother to throw a shoe through a window of the house next door and ended up with my grandfather shooting a patrolman. I am sorry, therefore, as I have said, that I ever paid any attention to the footsteps.

They began about a quarter past one o'clock in the morning, a rhythmic, quick-cadenced walking around the dining-room table. My mother was asleep in one room upstairs, my brother Herman in another; grandfather was in the attic, in the old walnut bed which, as you will remember, once fell on my father. I had just stepped out of the bathtub and was busily rubbing myself with a towel when I heard the steps. They were the steps of a man walking rapidly around the dining-room table downstairs. The light from the bathroom shone down the back steps, which dropped directly into the dining-room; I could see the faint shine of plates on the plate-rail; I couldn't see the table. The steps kept going round and round the table; at regular intervals a board creaked, when it was trod upon. I supposed at first that it was my father or my brother Roy, who had gone to Indianapolis but were expected home at any time. I suspected next that it was a burglar. It did not enter my mind until later that it was a ghost.

After the walking had gone on for perhaps three minutes, I tiptoed to Herman's room. "Psst!" I hissed, in the dark, shaking him. "Awp," he said, in the low, hopeless tone of a despondent beagle—he always half suspected that something would "get him" in the night. I told him who I was. "There's something downstairs!" I said. He got up and followed me to the head of the back staircase. We listened together. There was no sound. The steps had ceased. Herman looked at me in some alarm: I had only the bath towel around my waist. He wanted to go back to bed, but I gripped his arm. "There's something down there!" I said. Instantly the steps began again, circled the dining-room table like a man running, and started up the stairs toward us, heavily, two at a time. The light still shone palely down the stairs; we saw nothing coming; we only heard the steps. Herman rushed to his room and slammed the door. I slammed shut the door at the stairs top and held my knee against it. After a long minute, I slowly opened it again. There was nothing there. There was no sound. None of us ever heard the ghost again.

The slamming of the doors had aroused mother: she peered out of her room. "What on earth are you boys doing?" she demanded. Herman ventured out of his room. "Nothing," he said, gruffly, but he was, in color, a light green. "What was all that running around downstairs?" said mother. So she had heard the steps, too! We just looked at her. "Burglars!" she shouted, intuitively. I tried to quiet her by starting lightly downstairs.

"Come on, Herman," I said.

"I'll stay with mother," he said. "She's all excited."

I stepped back onto the landing.

"Don't either of you go a step," said mother. "We'll call the police." Since the phone was downstairs, I didn't see how

He always half suspected that something would get him.

we were going to call the police—nor did I want the police—but mother made one of her quick, incomparable decisions. She flung up a window of her bedroom which faced the bedroom windows of the house of a neighbor, picked up a shoe, and whammed it through a pane of glass across the narrow space that separated the two houses. Glass tinkled into the bedroom occupied by a retired engraver named Bodwell and his wife. Bodwell had been for some years in rather a bad way and was subject to mild "attacks." Most everybody we knew or lived near had *some* kind of attacks.

It was now about two o'clock of a moonless night; clouds hung black and low. Bodwell was at the window in a minute, shouting, frothing a little, shaking his fist. "We'll sell the house and go back to Peoria," we could hear Mrs. Bodwell saying. It was some time before mother "got through" to Bodwell. "Burglars!" she shouted. "Burglars in the house!" Herman and I hadn't dared to tell her that it was not burglars but ghosts, for she was even more afraid of ghosts than of burglars. Bodwell at first thought that she meant there were burglars in his house, but finally he quieted down and called the police for us over an extension phone by his bed. After he had disappeared from the window, mother suddenly made as if to throw another shoe, not because there was further need of it but, as she later explained, because the thrill of heaving a shoe through a window glass had enormously taken her fancy. I prevented her.

The police were on hand in a commendably short time: a Ford sedan full of them, two on motorcycles, and a patrol wagon with about eight in it and a few reporters. They began banging at our front door. Flashlights shot streaks of gleam up and down the walls, across the yard, down the walk between our house and Bodwell's. "Open up!" cried a hoarse voice. "We're men from Headquarters!" I wanted to go down and let them in, since there they were, but mother wouldn't hear of it. "You haven't a stitch on," she pointed out. "You'd catch your death." I wound the towel around me again. Finally the cops put their shoulders to our big heavy front door with its thick beveled glass and broke it in: I could hear a rending of wood and a splash of glass on the floor of the hall. Their lights played all over the living-room and crisscrossed nervously in the dining-room, stabbed into hallways, shot up the front stairs and finally up the back. They caught me standing in my towel at the top. A heavy policeman bounded up the steps. "Who are you?" he demanded. "I live here," I said. "Well, whattsa matta, ya hot?" he asked. It was, as a matter of fact, cold; I went to my room and pulled on some trousers. On my way out, a cop stuck a gun into my ribs. "Whatta you doin' here?" he demanded. "I live here," I said.

The officer in charge reported to mother. "No sign of nobody, lady," he said. "Musta got away—whatt'd he look like?" "There were two or three of them," mother said, "whooping and carrying on and slamming doors." "Funny," said the cop. "All ya windows and doors was locked on the inside tight as a tick."

Downstairs, we could hear the tromping of the other police. Police were all over the place; doors were yanked open, drawers were yanked open, windows were shot up and pulled down, furniture fell with dull thumps. A half-dozen policemen emerged out of the darkness of the front hallway upstairs. They began to ransack the floor: pulled beds away from walls, tore clothes off hooks in the closets, pulled suitcases and boxes off shelves. One of them found an old zither that Roy had won in a pool tournament. "Looky here, Joe," he said, strumming it with a big paw. The cop named Joe took it and turned it over. "What is it?" he asked me. "It's an old zither our guinea pig used to sleep on," I said. It was true that a pet guinea pig we once had would never sleep anywhere except on the zither, but I should never have said so. Joe and the other cop looked at me a long time. They put the zither back on a shelf.

"No sign o' nuthin'," said the cop who had first spoken to mother. "This guy," he explained to the others, jerking a

Police were all over the place.

thumb at me, "was nekked. The lady seems historical." They all nodded, but said nothing; just looked at me. In the small silence we all heard a creaking in the attic. Grandfather was turning over in bed. "What's 'at?" snapped Joe. Five or six cops sprang for the attic door before I could intervene or explain. I realized that it would be bad if they burst in on grandfather unannounced, or even announced. He was going through a phase in which he believed that General Meade's men, under steady hammering by Stonewall Jackson, were beginning to retreat and even desert.

When I got to the attic, things were pretty confused. Grandfather had evidently jumped to the conclusion that the police were deserters from Meade's army, trying to hide away in his attic. He bounded out of bed wearing a long flannel nightgown over long woolen underwear, a nightcap, and a leather jacket around his chest. The cops must have realized at once that the indignant white-haired old man belonged in the house, but they had no chance to say so. "Back, ye cowardly dogs!" roared grandfather. "Back t' the lines, ye goddam lily-livered cattle!" With that, he fetched the officer who found the zither a flat-handed smack alongside his head that sent him sprawling. The others beat a retreat, but not fast enough; grandfather grabbed Zither's gun from its holster and let fly. The report seemed to crack the rafters; smoke filled the attic. A cop cursed and shot his hand to his shoulder. Somehow, we all finally got downstairs again and locked the door against the old gentleman. He fired once or twice more in the darkness and then went back to bed. "That was grandfather," I explained to Joe, out of breath. "He thinks you're deserters." "I'll say he does," said Joe.

The cops were reluctant to leave without getting their hands on somebody besides grandfather; the night had been distinctly a defeat for them. Furthermore, they obviously didn't like the "layout"; something looked—and I can see their viewpoint—phony. They began to poke into things again. A reporter, a thin-faced, wispy man, came up to me. I had put on one of mother's blouses, not being able to find anything else. The reporter looked at me with mingled suspicion and interest. "Just what the hell is the real lowdown here, Bud?" he asked. I decided to be frank with him. "We had ghosts," I said. He gazed at me a long time as if I were a slot machine into which he had, without results, dropped a nickel. Then he walked away. The cops followed him, the one grandfather shot holding his now-bandaged arm, cursing and blaspheming. "I'm gonna get my gun back from that old bird," said the zither-cop. "Yeh," said Joe. "You—and who else?" I told them I would bring it to the station house the next day.

"What was the matter with that one policeman?" mother asked, after they had gone. "Grandfather shot him," I said. "What for?" she demanded. I told her he was a deserter. "Of all things!" said mother. "He was such a nice-looking young man."

Grandfather was fresh as a daisy and full of jokes at breakfast next morning. We thought at first he had forgotten all about what had happened, but he hadn't. Over his third cup of coffee, he glared at Herman and me. "What was the idee of all them cops tarryhootin' round the house last night?" he demanded. He had us there.

5

More Alarms at Night

One of the incidents that I always think of first when I cast back over my youth is what happened the night that my father "threatened to get Buck." This, as you will see, is not precisely a fair or accurate description of what actually occurred, but it is the way in which I and the other members of my family invariably allude to the occasion. We were living at the time in an old house at 77 Lexington Avenue, in Columbus, Ohio. In the early years of the nineteenth century, Columbus won out, as state capital, by only one vote over Lancaster, and ever since then has had the hallucination that it is being followed, a curious municipal state of mind which affects, in some way or other, all those who live there. Columbus is a town in which almost anything is likely to happen and in which almost everything has.

My father was sleeping in the front room on the second floor next to that of my brother Roy, who was then about sixteen. Father was usually in bed by nine-thirty and up again by ten-thirty to protest bitterly against a Victrola record we three boys were in the habit of playing over and over, namely, "No News, or What Killed the Dog," a recitation by Nat Wills. The record had been played so many times that its grooves were deeply cut and the needle often kept revolving in the same groove, repeating over and over the same words. Thus: "ate some burnt hoss flesh, ate some burnt hoss flesh, ate some burn hoss flesh." It was this reiteration that generally got father out of bed.

On the night in question, however, we had all gone to bed at about the same time, without much fuss. Roy, as a matter of fact, had been in bed all day with a kind of mild fever. It wasn't severe enough to cause delirium and my brother was the last person in the world to give way to delirium. Nevertheless, he had warned father when father went to bed, that he *might* become delirious.

About three o'clock in the morning, Roy, who was wakeful, decided to pretend that delirium was on him, in order to have, as he later explained it, some "fun." He got out of bed and, going to my father's room, shook him and said, "Buck, your time has come!" My father's name was not Buck but Charles, nor had he ever been called Buck. He was a tall, mildly nervous, peaceable gentleman, given to quiet pleasures, and eager that everything should run smoothly. "Hmm?" he said, with drowsy bewilderment. "Get up, Buck," said my brother, coldly, but with a certain gleam in his eyes. My father leaped out of bed, on the side away from his son, rushed from the room, locked the door behind him, and shouted us all up.

We were naturally enough reluctant to believe that Roy, who was quiet and self-contained, had threatened his father with any such abracadabra as father said he had. My older brother, Herman, went back to bed without any comment. "You've had a bad dream," my mother said. This vexed my father. "I tell you he called me Buck and told me my time had come," he said. We went to the door of his room, unlocked it, and tiptoed through it to Roy's room. He lay in his bed, breathing easily, as if he were fast asleep. It was apparent at a glance that he did not have a high fever. My mother gave my father a look. "I tell you he did," whispered father.

Our presence in the room finally seemed to awaken Roy and he was (or rather, as we found out long afterward, pretended to be) astonished and bewildered. "What's the matter?" he asked. "Nothing," said my mother. "Just your father had a nightmare." "I did not have a nightmare," said father, slowly and firmly. He wore an old-fashioned, "side-slit" nightgown which looked rather odd on his tall, spare figure. The situation, before we let it drop and everybody went back to bed again, became, as such situations in our family usually did, rather more complicated than ironed out. Roy demanded to know what had happened, and my mother told him, in considerably garbled fashion, what father had told her. At this a light dawned in Roy's eyes. "Dad's got it backward," he said. He then explained that he had heard father get out of bed and had called to him. "I'll handle this," his father had answered. "Buck is downstairs." "Who is this Buck?" my mother demanded of father. "I don't know any Buck and I never said that," father contended, irritably. None of us (except Roy, of course) believed him. "You had a dream," said mother. "People have these dreams." "I did not have a dream," father said. He was pretty well nettled by this time, and he stood in front of a bureau mirror, brushing his hair with a pair of military brushes; it always seemed to calm father to brush his hair. My mother declared that it was "a sin and a shame" for a grown man to wake up a sick boy simply because he (the grown man: father) had got on his back and had a bad dream. My father, as a matter of fact, *had* been known to have nightmares, usually about Lillian Russell and President Cleveland, who chased him.

We argued the thing for perhaps another half-hour, after which mother made father sleep in her room. "You're all safe now, boys," she said, firmly, as she shut her door. I could hear father grumbling for a long time, with an occasional monosyllable of doubt from mother.

It was some six months after this that father went through

a similar experience with me. He was at that time sleeping in the room next to mine. I had been trying all afternoon, in vain, to think of the name Perth Amboy. It seems now like a very simple name to recall and yet on the day in question I thought of every other town in the country, as well as such words and names and phrases as terra cotta, Walla-Walla, bill of lading, vice versa, hoity-toity, Pall Mall, Bodley Head, Schumann-Heink, etc., without even coming close to Perth Amboy. I suppose terra cotta was the closest I came, although it was not very close.

Long after I had gone to bed, I was struggling with the problem. I began to indulge in the wildest fancies as I lay there in the dark, such as that there was no such town, and even that there was no such state as New Jersey. I fell to repeating the word "Jersey" over and over again, until it became idiotic and meaningless. If you have ever lain awake at night and repeated one word over and over, thousands and millions and hundreds of thousands of millions of times, you know the disturbing mental state you can get into. I got to thinking that there was nobody else in the world but me, and various other wild imaginings of that nature. Eventually, lying there thinking these outlandish thoughts, I grew slightly alarmed. I began to suspect that one might lose one's mind over some such trivial mental tic as a futile search for terra firma Piggly Wiggly Gorgonzola Prester John Arc de Triomphe Holy Moses Lares and Penates. I began to feel the imperative necessity of human contact. This silly and alarming tangle of thought and fancy had gone far enough. I might get into some kind of mental aberrancy unless I found out the name of that Jersey town and could go to sleep. Therefore, I got out of bed, walked into the room where father was sleeping, and shook him. "Um?" he mumbled. I shook him more fiercely and he finally woke up, with a glaze of dream and apprehension in his eyes. "What's matter?" he asked thickly. I must, indeed, have been rather wild of eye, and my hair, which is unruly, becomes monstrously tousled and snarled at night. "Wha's it?" said my father, sitting up, in readiness to spring out of bed on the far side. The thought must have been going through his mind that all his sons were crazy, or on the verge of going crazy. I see that now, but I didn't then, for I had forgotten the Buck incident and did not realize how similar my appearance must have been to Roy's the night he called father Buck and told him his time had come. "Listen," I said. "Name some towns in New Jersey quick!" It must have been around three in the morning. Father got up, keeping the bed between him and me, and started to pull his trousers on. "Don't bother about dressing," I said. "Just name some towns in New Jersey." While he hastily pulled on his clothes—I remember he left his socks off and put his shoes on his bare feet—father began to name, in a shaky voice, various New Jersey cities. I can still see him reaching for his coat without taking his eyes off me. "Newark," he said, "Jersey City, Atlantic City, Elizabeth, Paterson, Passaic, Trenton, Jersey City, Trenton, Paterson—" "It has two names," I snapped. "Elizabeth and Paterson," he said. "No, no!" I told him, irritably. "This is one town with one name, but there are two words in it, like helter-skelter." "Helter-skelter," said my father, moving slowly toward the bedroom door and smiling in a faint, strained way which I understand now—but didn't then—was meant to humor me. When he was within a few paces of the door, he fairly leaped for it and ran out into the hall, his coat-tails and shoelaces flying. The exit stunned me. I had no notion that he thought I had gone out of my senses; I could only believe that he had gone out of *his* or that, only partially awake, he was engaged in some form of running in his sleep. I ran after him and caught him at the door of mother's room and grabbed him, in order to reason with him. I shook him a little, thinking to wake him completely. "Mary! Roy! Herman!" he shouted. I, too, began to shout for my brothers and my mother. My mother opened her door instantly, and there we were at 3:30 in the morning grappling and shouting, father partly dressed, but without socks or shirt, and I in pajamas.

"*Now*, what?" demanded my mother, grimly, pulling us apart. She was capable, fortunately, of handling any two of us and she never in her life was alarmed by the words or actions of any one of us.

"Look out for Jamie!" said father. (He always called me Jamie when excited.) My mother looked at me.

"What's the matter with your father?" she demanded. I said I didn't know; I said he had got up suddenly and dressed and ran out of the room.

"Where did you think you were going?" mother asked him, coolly. He looked at me. We looked at each other, breathing hard, but somewhat calmer.

"He was babbling about New Jersey at this infernal hour of the night," said father. "He came to my room and asked me to name towns in New Jersey." Mother looked at me.

"I just asked him," I said. "I was trying to think of one and couldn't sleep."

"You see?" said father, triumphantly. Mother didn't look at him.

"Get to bed, both of you," she said. "I don't want to hear any more out of you tonight. Dressing and tearing up and down the hall at this hour in the morning!" She went back into the room and shut her door. Father and I went back to bed. "Are you all right?" he called to me. "Are you?" I asked. "Well, good night," he said. "Good night," I said.

Mother would not let the rest of us discuss the affair next morning at breakfast. Herman asked what the hell had been the matter. "We'll go on to something more elevating," said mother.

6

A Sequence of Servants

When I look back on the long line of servants my mother hired during the years I lived at home, I remember clearly ten or twelve of them (we had about a hundred and sixty-two, all told, but few of them were memorable). There was, among the immortals, Dora Gedd, a quiet, mousy girl of thirty-two who one night shot at a man in her room, throwing our household into an uproar that was equalled perhaps only by the goings-on the night the ghost got in. Nobody knew how her lover, a morose garage man, got into the house, but everybody for two blocks knew how he got out. Dora had dressed up in a lavender evening gown for the occasion and she wore a mass of jewelry, some of which was my mother's. She kept shouting something from Shakespeare after the shooting—I forget just what—and pursued the gentleman downstairs from her attic room. When he got to the second floor he rushed into my father's room. It was this entrance, and not the shot or the shouting, that aroused father, a deep sleeper always. "Get me out of here!" shouted the victim. This situation rapidly developed, from then on, into one of those bewildering involvements for which my family had, I am afraid, a kind of unhappy genius. When the cops arrived Dora was shooting out the

Welsbach gas mantles in the living room, and her gentleman friend had fled. By dawn everything was quiet once more.

There were others. Gertie Straub: big, genial, and ruddy, a collector of pints of rye (we learned after she was gone), who came in after two o'clock one night from a dancing party at Buckeye Lake and awakened us by bumping into and knocking over furniture. "Who's down there?" called mother from upstairs. "It's me, dearie," said Gertie, "Gertie Straub." "What are you *doing?*" demanded mother. "Dusting," said Gertie.

Juanemma Kramer was one of my favorites. Her mother loved the name Juanita so dearly that she worked the first part of it into the names of all her daughters—they were (in addition to a Juanita) Juanemma, Juanhelen, and Juangrace. Juanemma was a thin, nervous maid who lived in constant dread of being hypnotized. Nor were her fears unfounded, for she was so extremely susceptible to hypnotic suggestion that one evening at B. F. Keith's theatre when a man on the stage was hypnotized, Juanemma, in the audience, was hypnotized too and floundered out into the aisle making the same cheeping sound that the subject on the stage, who had been told he was a chicken, was making. The act was abandoned and some xylophone players were brought on to restore order. One night, when our house was deep in quiet slumber, Juanemma became hypnotized in her sleep. She dreamed that a man "put her under" and then disappeared without "bringing her out." This was explained when, at last, a police surgeon whom we called in—he was the only doctor we could persuade to come out at three in the morning—slapped her into consciousness. It got so finally that any buzzing or whirring sound or any flashing object would put Juanemma under, and we had to let her go. I was reminded of her recently when, at a performance of the movie "Rasputin and the Empress," there came the scene in which Lionel Barrymore as the unholy priest hypnotized the Czarevitch by spinning before her eyes a glittering watch. If Juanemma sat in any theatre and witnessed that scene

"Dusting," said Gertie.

she must, I am sure, have gone under instantly. Happily, she seems to have missed the picture, for otherwise Mr. Barrymore might have had to dress up again as Rasputin (which God forbid) and journey across the country to get her out of it—excellent publicity but a great bother.

Before I go on to Vashti, whose last name I forget, I will look in passing at another of our white maids (Vashti was a Negress). Belle Giddin distinguished herself by one gesture which fortunately did not result in the bedlam occasioned by Juanemma's hypnotic states or Dora Gedd's shooting spree. Belle burned her finger previously, and purposely, one afternoon in the steam of a boiling kettle so that she could find out whether the pain-killer she had bought one night at a tent-show for fifty cents was any good. It was only fair.

Vashti turned out, in the end, to be partly legendary. She was a comely and sombre Negress who was always able to find things my mother lost. "I don't know what's become of my garnet brooch," my mother said one day. "Yassum," said Vashti. In half an hour she had found it. "Where in the world was it?" asked mother. "In de yahd," said Vashti. "De dog mussa drug it out."

Vashti was in love with a young Negro chauffeur named Charley, but she was also desired by her stepfather, whom none of us had ever seen but who was, she said, a handsome but messin' round gentleman from Georgia who had come north and married Vashti's mother just so he could be near Vashti. Charley, her fiancé, was for killing the stepfather but we counselled flight to another city. Vashti, however, would burst into tears and hymns and vow she'd never leave us; she got a certain pleasure out of bearing her cross. Thus we all lived in jeopardy, for the possibility that Vashti, Charley, and her stepfather might fight it out some night in our kitchen did not, at times, seem remote. Once I went into the kitchen at midnight to make some coffee. Charley was standing at a window looking out into the backyard; Vashti was rolling her eyes.

"Heah he come! Heah he come!" she moaned. The stepfather didn't show up, however.

Charley finally saved up twenty-seven dollars toward taking Vashti away but one day he impulsively bought a .22 revolver with a mother-of-pearl handle and demanded that Vashti tell him where her mother and stepfather lived. "Doan go up dere, doan go *up* dere!" said Vashti. "Mah mothah is just as rarin' as he is!" Charley, however, insisted. It came out then that Vashti didn't have any stepfather; there was no such person. Charley threw her over for a yellow gal named Nancy: he never forgave Vashti for the vanishing from his life of a menace that had come to mean more to him than Vashti herself. Afterwards, if you asked Vashti about her stepfather or about Charley she would say, proudly, and with a woman-of-the-world air, "Neither one ob 'em is messin' round *me* any mo'."

Mrs. Doody, a huge, middle-aged woman with a religious taint, came into and went out of our house like a comet. The second night she was there she went berserk while doing the dishes and, under the impression that father was the Antichrist, pursued him several times up the backstairs and down the front. He had been sitting quietly over his coffee in the living room when she burst in from the kitchen waving a bread knife. My brother Herman finally felled her with a piece of Libby's cut-glass that had been a wedding present of mother's. Mother, I remember, was in the attic at that time, trying to find some old things, and, appearing on the scene in the midst of it all, got the quick and mistaken impression that father was chasing Mrs. Doody.

Mrs. Robertson, a fat and mumbly old Negro woman, who might have been sixty and who might have been a hundred, gave us more than one turn during the many years that she did our washing. She had been a slave down South and she remembered having seen the troops marching—"a mess o' blue, den a mess o' gray." "What," my mother asked her once, "were they fighting about?" "Dat," said Mrs. Robertson, "Ah

"One night while doing the dishes . . ."

don't know." She had a feeling, at all times, that something was going to happen. I can see her now, staggering up from the basement with a basketful of clothes and coming abruptly to a halt in the middle of the kitchen. "Hahk!" she would say, in a deep, guttural voice. We would all hark; there was never anything to be heard. Neither, when she shouted "Look yondah!" and pointed a trembling hand at a window, was there ever anything to be seen. Father protested time and again that he couldn't stand Mrs. Robertson around, but mother always refused to let her go. It seems that she was a jewel. Once she walked unbidden, a dishpan full of wrung-out clothes under her arm, into father's study, where he was engrossed in some figures. Father looked up. She regarded him for a moment in silence. Then—"Look out!" she said, and withdrew. Another time, a murky winter afternoon, she came flubbering up the cellar stairs and bounced, out of breath, into the kitchen. Father was in the kitchen sipping some black coffee; he was in a jittery state of nerves from the effects of having had a tooth out, and had been in bed most of the day. "Dey is a death watch downstaihs!" rumbled the old Negro lady. It developed that she had heard a strange "chipping" noise back of the furnace. "That was a cricket," said father. "Um-*hm*," said Mrs. Robertson. "Dat was uh death watch!" With that she put on her hat and went home, poising just long enough at the back door to observe darkly to father, *"Dey ain't no way!"* It upset him for days.

Mrs. Robertson had only one great hour that I can think of—Jack Johnson's victory over Mistah Jeffries on the Fourth of July, 1910. She took a prominent part in the Negro parade through the South End that night, playing a Spanish fandango on a banjo. The procession was led by the pastor of her church who, Mrs. Robertson later told us, had 'splained that the victory of Jack over Mistah Jeffries proved "de 'speriority ob de race." "What," asked my mother, "did he mean by that?" "Dat," said Mrs. Robertson, "Ah don't know."

Our other servants I don't remember so clearly, except the one who set the house on fire (her name eludes me), and Edda Millmoss. Edda was always slightly morose but she had gone along for months, all the time she was with us, quietly and efficiently attending to her work, until the night we had Carson Blair and F. R. Gardiner to dinner—both men of importance to my father's ambitions. Then suddenly, while serving the entrée, Edda dropped everything and, pointing a quivering finger at father, accused him in a long rigamarole of having done her out of her rights to the land on which Trinity Church in New York stands. Mr. Gardiner had one of his "attacks" and the whole evening turned out miserably

7

The Dog That Bit People

Probably no one man should have as many dogs in his life as I have had, but there was more pleasure than distress in them for me except in the case of an Airedale named Muggs. He gave me more trouble than all the other fifty-four or -five put together, although my moment of keenest embarrassment was the time a Scotch terrier named Jeannie, who had just had six puppies in the clothes closet of a fourth floor apartment in New York, had the unexpected seventh and last at the corner of Eleventh Street and Fifth Avenue during a walk she had insisted on taking. Then, too, there was the prize-winning French poodle, a great big black poodle—none of your little, untroublesome white miniatures—who got sick riding in the rumble seat of a car with me on her way to the Greenwich Dog Show. She had a red rubber bib tucked around her throat and, since a rain storm came up when we were half way through the Bronx, I had to hold over her a small green umbrella, really more of a parasol. The rain beat down fearfully and suddenly the driver of the car drove into a big garage, filled with mechanics. It happened so quickly that I forgot to put the umbrella down and I will always remember, with sickening distress, the look of incredulity mixed with hatred that came over the face of the particular hardened garage man that came over to see what we wanted, when he took a look at me and the poodle. All garage men, and people of that intolerant stripe, hate poodles with their curious hair cut, especially the pom-poms that you got to leave on their hips if you expect the dogs to win a prize.

But the Airedale, as I have said, was the worst of all my dogs. He really wasn't my dog, as a matter of fact: I came home from a vacation one summer to find that my brother Roy had bought him while I was away. A big, burly, choleric dog, he always acted as if he thought I wasn't one of the family. There was a slight advantage in being one of the family, for he didn't bite the family as often as he bit strangers. Still, in the years that we had him he bit everybody but mother, and he made a pass at her once but missed. That was during the month when we suddenly had mice, and Muggs refused to do anything about them. Nobody ever had mice exactly like the mice we had that month. They acted like pet mice, almost like mice somebody had trained. They were so friendly that one night when mother entertained at dinner the Friraliras, a club she and my father had belonged to for twenty years, she put down a lot of little dishes with food in them on the pantry floor so that the mice would be satisfied with that and wouldn't come into the dining room. Muggs stayed out in the pantry with the mice, lying on the floor, growling to himself—not at the mice, but about all the people in the next room that he would have liked to get at. Mother slipped out into the pantry once to see how everything was going. Everything was going fine. It made her so mad to see Muggs lying there, oblivious of the mice—they came running up to her—that she slapped him and he slashed at her, but didn't make it. He was sorry immediately, mother said. He was always sorry, she said, after he bit someone, but we could not understand how she figured this out. He didn't act sorry.

Mother used to send a box of candy every Christmas to the people the Airedale bit. The list finally contained forty or more names. Nobody could understand why we didn't get rid of the dog. I didn't understand it very well myself, but we didn't get rid of him. I think that one or two people tried to poison Muggs—he acted poisoned once in a while—and old Major Moberly fired at him once with his service revolver near the Seneca Hotel in East Broad Street—but Muggs lived to be almost eleven years old and even when he could hardly get around he bit a Congressman who had called to see my father on business. My mother had never liked the Congressman— she said the signs of his horoscope showed he couldn't be trusted (he was Saturn with the moon in Virgo)—but she sent him a box of candy that Christmas. He sent it right back, probably because he suspected it was trick candy. Mother persuaded herself it was all for the best that the dog had bitten him, even though father lost an important business association because of it. "I wouldn't be associated with such a man," mother said, "Muggs could read him like a book."

We used to take turns feeding Muggs to be on his good side, but that didn't always work. He was never in a very good humor, even after a meal. Nobody knew exactly what was the matter with him, but whatever it was it made him irascible, especially in the mornings. Roy never felt very well in the morning, either, especially before breakfast, and once when he came downstairs and found that Muggs had moodily chewed up the morning paper he hit him in the face with a grapefruit and then jumped up on the dining-room table, scattering dishes and silverware and spilling the coffee. Muggs' first free leap carried him all the way across the table and into a brass fire screen in front of the gas grate but he was back on his feet in a moment and in the end he got Roy and gave him a pretty vicious bite in the leg. Then he was all over it; he never bit anyone more than once at a time. Mother always mentioned that as an argument in his favor; she said he had a quick temper but that he didn't hold a grudge. She was forever defending him. I think she liked him because he wasn't well. "He's not

Nobody knew exactly what was the matter with him.

strong," she would say, pityingly, but that was inaccurate; he may not have been well but he was terribly strong.

One time my mother went to the Chittenden Hotel to call on a woman mental healer who was lecturing in Columbus on the subject of "Harmonious Vibrations." She wanted to find out if it was possible to get harmonious vibrations into a dog. "He's a large tan-colored Airedale," mother explained. The woman said that she had never treated a dog but she advised my mother to hold the thought that he did not bite and would not bite. Mother was holding the thought the very next morning when Muggs got the iceman but she blamed that slip-up on the iceman. "If you didn't think he would bite you, he wouldn't," mother told him. He stomped out of the house in a terrible jangle of vibrations.

One morning when Muggs bit me slightly, more or less in passing, I reached down and grabbed his short stumpy tail and hoisted him into the air. It was a foolhardy thing to do and the last time I saw my mother, about six months ago, she said she didn't know what possessed me. I don't either, except that I was pretty mad. As long as I held the dog off the floor by his tail he couldn't get at me, but he twisted and jerked so, snarling all the time, that I realized I couldn't hold him that way very long. I carried him to the kitchen and flung him onto the floor and shut the door on him just as he crashed against it. But I forgot about the backstairs. Muggs went up the back-stairs and down the frontstairs and had me cornered in the living room. I managed to get up onto the mantelpiece above the fireplace, but it gave way and came down with a tremendous crash throwing a large marble clock, several vases, and myself heavily to the floor. Muggs was so alarmed by the racket that when I picked myself up he had disappeared. We couldn't find him anywhere, although we whistled and shouted, until old Mrs. Detweiler called after dinner that night. Muggs had bitten her once, in the leg, and she came into the living room only after we assured her that Muggs had run away. She had

Lots of people reported our dog to the police.

just seated herself when, with a great growling and scratching of claws, Muggs emerged from under a davenport where he had been quietly hiding all the time, and bit her again. Mother examined the bite and put arnica on it and told Mrs. Detweiler that it was only a bruise. "He just bumped you," she said. But Mrs. Detweiler left the house in a nasty state of mind.

Lots of people reported our Airedale to the police but my father held a municipal office at the time and was on friendly terms with the police. Even so, the cops had been out a couple of times—once when Muggs bit Mrs. Rufus Sturtevant and again when he bit Lieutenant-Governor Malloy—but mother told them that it hadn't been Muggs' fault but the fault of the people who were bitten. "When he starts for them, they scream," she explained, "and that excites him." The cops suggested that it might be a good idea to tie the dog up, but mother said that it mortified him to be tied up and that he wouldn't eat when he was tied up.

Muggs at his meals was an unusual sight. Because of the fact that if you reached toward the floor he would bite you, we usually put his food plate on top of an old kitchen table with a bench alongside the table. Muggs would stand on the bench and eat. I remember that my mother's Uncle Horatio, who boasted that he was the third man up Missionary Ridge, was splutteringly indignant when he found out that we fed the dog on a table because we were afraid to put his plate on the floor. He said he wasn't afraid of any dog that ever lived and that he would put the dog's plate on the floor if we would give it to him. Roy said that if Uncle Horatio had fed Muggs on the ground just before the battle he would have been the first man up Missionary Ridge. Uncle Horatio was furious. "Bring him in! Bring him in now!" he shouted. "I'll feed the —— on the floor!" Roy was all for giving him a chance, but my father wouldn't hear of it. He said that Muggs had already been fed. "I'll feed him again!" bawled Uncle Horatio. We had quite a time quieting him.

Muggs at his meals was an unusual sight.

In his last year Muggs used to spend practically all of his time outdoors. He didn't like to stay in the house for some reason or other—perhaps it held too many unpleasant memories for him. Anyway, it was hard to get him to come in and as a result the garbage man, the iceman, and the laundryman wouldn't come near the house. We had to haul the garbage down to the corner, take the laundry out and bring it back, and meet the iceman a block from home. After this had gone on for some time wc hit on an ingenious arrangement for getting the dog in the house so that we could lock him up while the gas meter was read, and so on. Muggs was afraid of only one thing, an electrical storm. Thunder and lightning frightened him out of his senses (I think he thought a storm had broken the day the mantelpiece fell). He would rush into the house and hide under a bed or in a clothes closet. So we fixed up a thunder machine out of a long narrow piece of sheet iron with a wooden handle on one end. Mother would shake this vigorously when she wanted to get Muggs into the house. It made an excellent imitation of thunder, but I suppose it was the most round-about system for running a household that was ever devised. It took a lot out of mother.

A few months before Muggs died, he got to "seeing things." He would rise slowly from the floor, growling low, and stalk stiff-legged and menacing toward nothing at all. Sometimes the Thing would be just a little to the right or left of a visitor. Once a Fuller Brush salesman got hysterics. Muggs came wandering into the room like Hamlet following his father's ghost. His eyes were fixed on a spot just to the left of the Fuller Brush man, who stood it until Muggs was about three slow, creeping paces from him. Then he shouted. Muggs wavered on past him into the hallway grumbling to himself but the Fuller man went on shouting. I think mother had to throw a pan of cold water on him before he stopped. That was the way she used to stop us boys when we got into fights.

Muggs died quite suddenly one night. Mother wanted to

bury him in the family lot under a marble stone with some such inscription as "Flights of angels sing thee to thy rest" but we persuaded her it was against the law. In the end we just put up a smooth board above his grave along a lonely road. On the board I wrote with an indelible pencil "Cave Canem." Mother was quite pleased with the simple classic dignity of the old Latin epitaph.

8

University Days

I passed all the other courses that I took at my University, but I could never pass botany. This was because all botany students had to spend several hours a week in a laboratory looking through a microscope at plant cells, and I could never see through a microscope. I never once saw a cell through a microscope. This used to enrage my instructor. He would wander around the laboratory pleased with the progress all the students were making in drawing the involved and, so I am told, interesting structure of flower cells, until he came to me. I would just be standing there. "I can't see anything," I would say. He would begin patiently enough, explaining how anybody can see through a microscope, but he would always end up in a fury, claiming that I could *too* see through a microscope but just pretended that I couldn't. "It takes away from the beauty of flowers anyway," I used to tell him. "We are not concerned with beauty in this course," he would say. "We are concerned solely with what I may call the *mechanics* of flars." "Well," I'd say, "I can't see anything." "Try it just once again," he'd say, and I would put my eye to the microscope and see nothing at all, except now and again a nebulous milky substance—a phenomenon of maladjustment. You were supposed to see a vivid, restless clockwork of sharply defined plant cells. "I see what looks like a lot of milk," I would tell him. This, he claimed, was the result of my not having adjusted the microscope properly, so he would readjust it for me, or rather, for himself. And I would look again and see milk.

I finally took a deferred pass, as they called it, and waited a year and tried again. (You had to pass one of the biological sciences or you couldn't graduate.) The professor had come back from vacation brown as a berry, bright-eyed, and eager to explain cell-structure again to his classes. "Well," he said to me, cheerily, when we met in the first laboratory hour of the semester, "we're going to see cells this time, aren't we?" "Yes, sir," I said. Students to right of me and to left of me and in front of me were seeing cells; what's more, they were quietly drawing pictures of them in their notebooks. Of course, I didn't see anything.

"We'll try it," the professor said to me, grimly, "with every adjustment of the microscope known to man. As God is my witness, I'll arrange this glass so that you see cells through it or I'll give up teaching. In twenty-two years of botany, I—" He cut off abruptly for he was beginning to quiver all over, like Lionel Barrymore, and he genuinely wished to hold onto his temper; his scenes with me had taken a great deal out of him.

So we tried it with every adjustment of the microscope known to man. With only one of them did I see anything but blackness or the familiar lacteal opacity, and that time I saw, to my pleasure and amazement, a variegated constellation of flecks, specks, and dots. These I hastily drew. The instructor, noting my activity, came back from an adjoining desk, a smile on his lips and his eyebrows high in hope. He looked at my cell drawing. "What's that?" he demanded, with a hint of a squeal in his voice. "That's what I saw," I said. "You didn't, you didn't, you *did*n't!" he screamed, losing control of his temper instantly, and he bent over and squinted into the micro-

He was beginning to quiver all over like Lionel Barrymore.

scope. His head snapped up. "That's your eye!" he shouted. "You've fixed the lens so that it reflects! You've drawn your eye!"

Another course that I didn't like, but somehow managed to pass, was economics. I went to that class straight from the botany class, which didn't help me any in understanding either subject. I used to get them mixed up. But not as mixed up as another student in my economics class who came there direct from a physics laboratory. He was a tackle on the football team, named Bolenciecwcz. At that time Ohio State University had one of the best football teams in the country, and Bolenciecwcz was one of its outstanding stars. In order to be eligible to play it was necessary for him to keep up in his studies, a very difficult matter, for while he was not dumber than an ox he was not any smarter. Most of his professors were lenient and helped him along. None gave him more hints, in answering questions, or asked him simpler ones than the economics professor, a thin, timid man named Bassum. One day when we were on the subject of transportation and distribution, it came Bolenciecwcz's turn to answer a question. "Name one means of transportation," the profession said to him. No light came into the big tackle's eyes. "Just any means of transportation," said the professor. Bolenciecwcz sat staring at him. "That is," pursued the professor, "any medium, agency, or method of going from one place to another." Bolenciecwcz had the look of a man who is being led into a trap. "You may choose among steam, horse-drawn, or electrically propelled vehicles," said the instructor. "I might suggest the one which we commonly take in making long journeys across land." There was a profound silence in which everybody stirred uneasily, including Bolenciecwcz and Mr. Bassum. Mr. Bassum abruptly broke this silence in an amazing manner. "Choo-choo-choo," he said, in a low voice, and turned instantly scarlet. He glanced appealingly around the room. All of us, of course, shared Mr. Bassum's desire that Bolenciecwcz should stay abreast of the class in economics, for the Illinois game, one of the hardest and most important of the season, was only a week off. "Toot, toot, too-tooooooot!" some student with a deep voice moaned, and we all looked encouragingly at Bolenciecwcz. Somebody else gave a fine imitation of a locomotive letting off steam. Mr. Bassum himself rounded off the little show. "Ding, dong, ding, dong," he said, hopefully. Bolenciecwcz was staring at the floor now, trying to think, his great brow furrowed, his huge hands rubbing together, his face red.

"How did you come to college this year, Mr. Bolenciecwcz?" asked the professor. "*Chuf*fa chuffa, *chuf*fa chuffa."

"M'father sent me," said the football player.

"What on?" asked Bassum.

"I git an 'lowance," said the tackle, in a low, husky voice, obviously embarrassed.

"No, no," said Bassum. "Name a means of transportation. What did you *ride* here on?"

"Train," said Bolenciecwcz.

"Quite right," said the professor. "Now, Mr. Nugent, will you tell us——"

If I went through anguish in botany and economics—for different reasons—gymnasium work was even worse. I don't even like to think about it. They wouldn't let you play games or join in the exercises with your glasses on and I couldn't see with mine off. I bumped into professors, horizontal bars, agricultural students, and swinging iron rings. Not being able to see, I could take it but I couldn't dish it out. Also, in order to pass gymnasium (and you had to pass it to graduate) you had to learn to swim if you didn't know how. I didn't like the swimming pool, I didn't like swimming, and I didn't like the swimming instructor, and after all these years I still don't. I never swam but I passed my gym work anyway, by having another student give my gymnasium number (978) and swim across the pool in my place. He was a quiet, amiable blonde youth, number 473, and he would have seen through a micro-

Bolenciecwcz was trying to think.

scope for me if we could have got away with it, but we couldn't get away with it. Another thing I didn't like about gymnasium work was that they made you strip the day you registered. It is impossible for me to be happy when I am stripped and being asked a lot of questions. Still, I did better than a lanky agricultural student who was cross-examined just before I was. They asked each student what college he was in—that is, whether Arts, Engineering, Commerce, or Agriculture. "What college are you in?" the instructor snapped at the youth in front of me. "Ohio State University," he said promptly.

It wasn't that agricultural student but it was another a whole lot like him who decided to take up journalism, possibly on the ground that when farming went to hell he could fall back on newspaper work. He didn't realize, of course, that that would be very much like falling back full-length on a kit of carpenter's tools. Haskins didn't seem cut out for journalism, being too embarrassed to talk to anybody and unable to use a typewriter, but the editor of the college paper assigned him to the cow barns, the sheep house, the horse pavilion, and the animal husbandry department generally. This was a genuinely big "beat," for it took up five times as much ground and got ten times as great a legislative appropriation as the College of Liberal Arts. The agricultural student knew animals, but nevertheless his stories were dull and colorlessly written. He took all afternoon on each of them, on account of having to hunt for each letter on the typewriter. Once in a while he had to ask somebody to help him hunt. "C" and "L," in particular, were hard letters for him to find. His editor finally got pretty much annoyed at the farmer-journalist because his pieces were so uninteresting. "See here, Haskins," he snapped at him one day, "Why is it we never have anything hot from you on the horse pavilion? Here we have two hundred head of horses on this campus—more than any other university in the Western Conference except Purdue—and yet you never get any real lowdown on them. Now shoot over to the horse barns and dig up something lively." Haskins shambled out and came back in about an hour; he said he had something. "Well, start it off snappily," said the editor. "Something people will read." Haskins set to work and in a couple of hours brought a sheet of typewritten paper to the desk; it was a two-hundred-word story about some disease that had broken out among the horses. Its opening sentence was simple but arresting. It read: "Who has noticed the sores on the tops of the horses in the animal husbandry building?"

Ohio State was a land grant university and therefore two years of military drill was compulsory. We drilled with old Springfield rifles and studied the tactics of the Civil War even though the World War was going on at the time. At 11 o'clock each morning thousands of freshmen and sophomores used to deploy over the campus, moodily creeping up on the old chemistry building. It was good training for the kind of warfare that was waged at Shiloh but it had no connection with what was going on in Europe. Some people used to think there was German money behind it, but they didn't dare say so or they would have been thrown in jail as German spies. It was a period of muddy thought and marked, I believe, the decline of higher education in the Middle West.

As a soldier I was never any good at all. Most of the cadets were glumly indifferent soldiers, but I was no good at all. Once General Littlefield, who was commandant of the cadet corps, popped up in front of me during regimental drill and snapped, "You are the main trouble with this university!" I think he meant that my type was the main trouble with the university but he may have meant me individually. I was mediocre at drill, certainly—that is, until my senior year. By that time I had drilled longer than anybody else in the Western Conference, having failed at military at the end of each preceding year so that I had to do it all over again. I was the only senior still in uniform. The uniform which, when new, had made me look like an interurban railway conductor, now that it had become

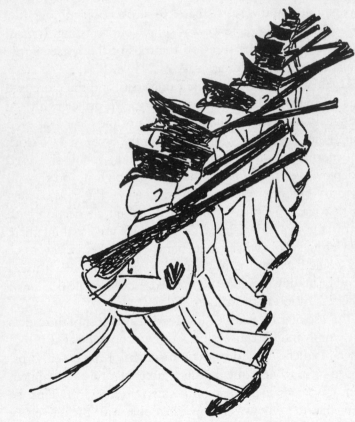

We drilled with old Springfield rifles.

faded and too tight made me look like Bert Williams in his bellboy act. This had a definitely bad effect on my morale. Even so, I had become by sheer practise little short of wonderful at squad manoeuvres.

One day General Littlefield picked our company out of the whole regiment and tried to get it mixed up by putting it through one movement after another as fast as we could execute them: squads right, squads left, squads on right into line, squads right about, squads left front into line, etc. In about three minutes one hundred and nine men were marching in one direction and I was marching away from them at an angle of forty degrees, all alone. "Company, halt!" shouted General Littlefield, "That man is the only man who has it right!" I was made a corporal for my achievement.

The next day General Littlefield summoned me to his office. He was swatting flies when I went in. I was silent and he was silent too, for a long time. I don't think he remembered me or why he had sent for me, but he didn't want to admit it. He swatted some more flies, keeping his eyes on them narrowly before he let go with the swatter. "Button up your coat!" he snapped. Looking back on it now I can see that he meant me although he was looking at a fly, but I just stood there. Another fly came to rest on a paper in front of the general and began rubbing its hind legs together. The general lifted the swatter cautiously. I moved restlessly and the fly flew away. "You startled him!" barked General Littlefield, looking at me severely. I said I was sorry. "That won't help the situation!" snapped the general, with cold military logic. I didn't see what I could do except offer to chase some more flies toward his desk, but I didn't say anything. He stared out the window at the faraway figures of co-eds crossing the campus toward the library. Finally, he told me I could go. So I went. He either didn't know which cadet I was or else he forgot what he wanted to see me about. It may have been that he wished to apologize for having called me the main trouble with the university; or maybe he had decided to compliment me on my brilliant drilling of the day before and then at the last minute decided not to. I don't know. I don't think about it much any more.

9

Draft Board Nights

I left the University in June, 1918, but I couldn't get into the army on account of my sight, just as grandfather couldn't get in on account of his age. He applied several times and each time he took off his coat and threatened to whip the men who said he was too old. The disappointment of not getting to Germany (he saw no sense in everybody going to France) and the strain of running around town seeing influential officials finally got him down in bed. He had wanted to lead a division and his chagrin at not even being able to enlist as a private was too much for him. His brother Jake, some fifteen years younger than he was, sat up at night with him after he took to bed, because we were afraid he might leave the house without even putting on his clothes. Grandfather was against the idea of Jake watching over him—he thought it was a lot of tomfoolery— but Jake hadn't been able to sleep at night for twenty-eight years, so he was the perfect person for such a vigil.

On the third night, grandfather was wakeful. He would open his eyes, look at Jake, and close them again, frowning. He never answered any question Jake asked him. About four o'clock that morning, he caught his brother sound asleep in the big leather chair beside the bed. When once Jake did fall asleep he slept deeply, so that grandfather was able to get up, dress himself, undress Jake, and put him in bed without waking him. When my Aunt Florence came into the room at seven o'clock, grandfather was sitting in the chair reading the *Memoirs of U.S. Grant* and Jake was sleeping in the bed. "He watched while I slept," said grandfather, "so now I'm watchin' while he sleeps." It seemed fair enough.

One reason we didn't want grandfather to roam around at night was that he had said something once or twice about going over to Lancaster, his old home town, and putting his problem up to "Cump"—that is, General William Tecumseh Sherman, also an old Lancaster boy. We knew that his inability to find Sherman would be bad for him and we were afraid that he might try to get there in the little electric runabout that had been bought for my grandmother. She had become, surprisingly enough, quite skilful at getting around town in it. Grandfather was astonished and a little indignant when he saw her get into the contraption and drive off smoothly and easily. It was her first vehicular triumph over him in almost fifty years of married life and he determined to learn to drive the thing himself. A famous old horseman, he approached it as he might have approached a wild colt. His brow would darken and he would begin to curse. He always leaped into it quickly, as if it might pull out from under him if he didn't get into the seat fast enough. The first few times he tried to run the electric, he went swiftly around in a small circle, drove over the curb, across the sidewalk, and up onto the lawn. We all tried to persuade him to give up, but his spirit was aroused. "Git that goddam buggy back in the road!" he would say, imperiously. So we would manoeuvre it back into the street and he would try again. Pulling too savagely on the guiding-bar—to teach the electric a lesson—was what took him around in a circle, and it was difficult to make him understand that it was best to relax and not get mad. He had the notion that if you didn't hold her, she would throw you. And a man who (or so he

About four o'clock he caught his brother asleep.

often told us) had driven a four-horse McCormick reaper when he was five years old did not intend to be thrown by an electric runabout.

Since there was no way of getting him to give up learning to operate the electric, we would take him out to Franklin Park, where the roadways were wide and unfrequented, and spend an hour or so trying to explain the differences between driving a horse and carriage and driving an electric. He would keep muttering all the time; he never got it out of his head that when he took the driver's seat the machine flattened its ears on him, so to speak. After a few weeks, nevertheless, he got so he could run the electric for a hundred yards or so along a fairly straight line. But whenever he took a curve, he invariably pulled or pushed the bar too quickly and too hard and headed for a tree or a flower bed. Someone was always with him and we would never let him take the car out of the park.

One morning when grandmother was all ready to go to market, she called the garage and told them to send the electric around. They said that grandfather had already been there and taken it out. There was a tremendous to-do. We telephoned Uncle Will and he got out his Lozier and we started off to hunt for grandfather. It was not yet seven o'clock and there was fortunately little traffic. We headed for Franklin Park, figuring that he might have gone out there to try to break the car's spirit. One or two early pedestrians had seen a tall old gentleman with a white beard driving a little electric and cussing as he drove. We followed a tortuous trail and found them finally on Nelson Road, about four miles from the town of Shepard. Grandfather was standing in the road shouting, and the back wheels of the electric were deeply entangled in a barbed-wire fence. Two workmen and a farmhand were trying to get the thing loose. Grandfather was in a state of high wrath about the electric. "The —— — —— backed up on me!" he told us.

But to get back to the war. The Columbus draft board never called grandfather for service, which was a lucky thing

There was a tremendous-to-do.

for them because they would have had to take him. There were
stories that several old men of eighty or ninety had been summoned in the confusion, but somehow or other grandfather
was missed. He waited every day for the call, but it never came.
My own experience was quite different. I was called almost
every week, even though I had been exempted from service the
first time I went before the medical examiners. Either they
were never convinced that it was me or else there was some
clerical error in the records which was never cleared up. Anyway, there was usually a letter for me on Monday ordering me
to report for examination on the second floor of Memorial
Hall the following Wednesday at 9 P.M. The second time I
went up, I tried to explain to one of the doctors that I had
already been exempted. "You're just a blur to me." I said, taking off my glasses. "You're absolutely nothing to me," he
snapped, sharply.

I had to take off all my clothes each time and jog around
the hall with a lot of porters and bank presidents' sons and
clerks and poets. Our hearts and lungs would be examined,
and then our feet; and finally our eyes. That always came last.
When the eye specialist got around to me, he would always
say, "Why, you couldn't get into the service with sight like
that!" "I know," I would say. Then a week or two later I would
be summoned again and go through the same rigmarole. The
ninth or tenth time I was called, I happened to pick up one of
several stethoscopes that were lying on a table and suddenly,
instead of finding myself in the line of draft men, I found
myself in the line of examiners. "Hello, doctor," said one of
them, nodding. "Hello," I said. That, of course, was before I
took my clothes off; I might have managed it naked, but I
doubt it. I was assigned, or rather drifted, to the chest-and-
lung section, where I began to examine every other man, thus
cutting old Dr. Ridgeway's work in two. "I'm glad to have you
here, doctor," he said.

I passed most of the men that came to me, but now and

then I would exempt one just to be on the safe side. I began by making each of them hold his breath and then say "mi, mi, mi, mi," until I noticed Ridgeway looking at me curiously. He, I discovered, simply made them say "ah," and some times he didn't make them say anything. Once I got hold of a man who, it came out later, had swallowed a watch—to make the doctors believe there was something wrong with him inside (it was a common subterfuge: men swallowed nails, hairpins, ink, etc., in an effort to be let out). Since I didn't know what you were supposed to hear through a stethoscope, the ticking of the watch at first didn't surprise me, but I decided to call Dr. Ridgeway into consultation, because nobody else had ticked. "This man seems to tick," I said to him. He looked at me in surprise but didn't say anything. Then he thumped the man, laid his ear to his chest, and finally tried the stethoscope. "Sound as a dollar," he said. "Listen lower down," I told him. The man indicated his stomach. Ridgeway gave him a haughty, indignant look. "That is for the abdominal men to worry about," he said, and moved off. A few minutes later, Dr. Blythe Ballomy got around to the man and listened, but he didn't blink an eye; his grim expression never changed. "You have swallowed a watch, my man," he said, crisply. The draftee reddened in embarrassment and uncertainty. "On *purpose*?" he asked. "That I can't say," the doctor told him, and went on.

I served with the draft board for about four months. Until the summonses ceased, I couldn't leave town and as long as I stayed and appeared promptly for examination, even though I did the examining, I felt that technically I could not be convicted of evasion. During the daytime, I worked as publicity agent for an amusement park, the manager of which was a tall, unexpected young man named Byron Landis. Some years before, he had dynamited the men's lounge in the statehouse annex for a prank; he enjoyed pouring buckets of water on sleeping persons, and once he had barely escaped arrest by

An abdominal man worrying.

jumping off the top of the old Columbus Transfer Company building with a homemade parachute.

He asked me one morning if I would like to take a ride in the new Scarlet Tornado, a steep and wavy roller-coaster. I didn't want to but I was afraid he would think I was afraid, so I went along. It was about ten o'clock and there was nobody at the park except workmen and attendants and concessionaires in their shirtsleeves. We climbed into one of the long gondolas of the roller-coaster and while I was looking around for the man who was going to run it, we began to move off. Landis, I discovered, was running it himself. But it was too late to get out; we had begun to climb, clickety-clockety, up the first steep incline, down the other side of which we careened at eighty miles an hour. "I didn't know you could run this thing!" I bawled at my companion, as we catapulted up a sixty-degree arch and looped headlong into space. "I didn't either!" he bawled back. The racket and the rush of air were terrific as we roared into the pitch-black Cave of Darkness and came out and down Monohan's Leap, so called because a workman named Monohan had been forced to jump from it when caught between two approaching experimental cars while it was being completed. That trip, although it ended safely, made a lasting impression on me. It is not too much to say that it has flavored my life. It is the reason I shout in my sleep, refuse to ride on the elevated, keep jerking the emergency brake in cars other people are driving, have the sensation of flying like a bird when I first lie down, and in certain months can't keep anything on my stomach.

During my last few trips to the draft board, I went again as a draft prospect, having grown tired of being an examiner. None of the doctors who had been my colleagues for so long recognized me, not even Dr. Ridgeway. When he examined my chest for the last time, I asked him if there hadn't been another doctor helping him. He said there had been. "Did he look anything like me?" I asked. Dr. Ridgeway looked at me.

"I don't think so," he said, "he was taller." (I had my shoes off while he was examining me.) "A good pulmonary man," added Ridgeway. "Relative of yours?" I said yes. He sent me on to Dr. Quimby, the specialist who had examined my eyes twelve or fifteen times before. He gave me some simple reading tests. "You could never get into the army with eyes like that," he said. "I know," I told him.

Late one morning, shortly after my last examination, I was awakened by the sound of bells ringing and whistles blowing. It grew louder and more insistent and wilder. It was the Armistice.

A Note at the End

The hard times of my middle years I pass over, leaving the ringing bells of 1918, with all their false promise, to mark the end of a special sequence. The sharp edges of old reticences are softened in the autobiographer by the passing of time—a man does not pull the pillow over his head when he wakes in the morning because he suddenly remembers some awful thing that happened to him fifteen or twenty years ago, but the confusions and the panics of last year and the year before are too close for contentment. Until a man can quit talking loudly to himself in order to shout down the memories of blunderings and gropings, he is in no shape for the painstaking examination of distress and the careful ordering of events so necessary to a calm and balanced exposition of what, exactly, was the matter. The time I fell out of the gun room in Mr. James Stanley's house in Green Lake, New York, is for instance, much too near for me to go into with any peace of mind, although it happened in 1925, the illfated year of "Horses, Horses, Horses" and "Valencia." There is now, I understand, a porch to walk out onto when you open the door I opened that night, but there wasn't then.

The mistaken exits and entrances of my thirties have moved me several times to some thought of spending the rest of my days wandering aimlessly around the South Seas, like a character out of Conrad, silent and inscrutable. But the necessity for frequent visits to my oculist and dentist has prevented this. You can't be running back from Singapore every few months to get your lenses changed and still retain the proper mood for wandering. Furthermore, my horn-rimmed glasses and my Ohio accent betray me, even when I sit on the terraces of little tropical cafes, wearing a pith helmet, staring straight ahead, and twitching a muscle in my jaw. I found this out when I tried wandering around the West Indies one summer. Instead of being followed by the whispers of men and the glances of women, I was followed by bead salesmen and native women with postcards. Nor did any dark girl, looking at all like Tondelayo in "White Cargo," come forward and offer to go to pieces with me. They tried to sell me baskets.

Under these circumstances it is impossible to be inscrutable and a wanderer who isn't inscrutable might just as well be

They tried to sell me baskets.

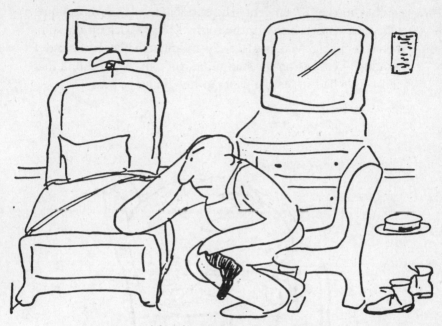

A hotel room in Louisville.

back at Broad and High Streets in Columbus sitting in the Baltimore Dairy Lunch. Nobody from Columbus has ever made a first rate wanderer in the Conradean tradition. Some of them have been fairly good at disappearing for a few days to turn up in a hotel in Louisville with a bad headache and no recollection of how they got there, but they always scurry back to their wives with some cock-and-bull story of having lost their memory or having gone away to attend the annual convention of the Fraternal Order of Eagles.

There was, of course, even for Conrad's Lord Jim, no running away. The cloud of his special discomfiture followed him like a pup, no matter what ships he took or what wilderness he entered. In the pathways between office and home and home and the houses of settled people there are always, ready to snap at you, the little perils of routine living, but there is no escape in the unplanned tangent, the sudden turn. In Martinique, when the whistle blew for the tourists to get back on the ship, I had a quick, wild, and lovely moment when I decided I wouldn't get back on the ship. I did, though. And I found that somebody had stolen the pants to my dinner jacket.

Afterword

He Knew When to Stop

The Thurber House in Columbus, Ohio, is just one of several houses the Thurber family occupied at various times in that city. It was chosen to be The Thurber House because, for one thing, nothing vital to American literature happened in the others, which in any case had long since gone to ruin.

This one was close to ruin when the forces of civilization, which in Columbus are robust and zealous, stepped in with the money and ideas needed to put it back together.

This is one of the more important houses in American letters. It is the house where the bed fell down and where the ghost got in.

These were what the book reviewers call "seminal" events in American letters. "Seminal" means something or somebody got seeded by them. What the intrusive ghost and the falling bed seeded was possibly the shortest and most elegant autobiography ever written: "My Life and Hard Times," by James Thurber.

The hard times recollected by Thurber ended circa 1918 when he was 24 years old. Though middle-aged when he wrote it, he sensibly declined to write about his mature years.

"The sharp edges of old reticences are softened in the autobiographer by the passing of time," he explained. "A man does not pull the pillow over his head when he wakes in the morning because he suddenly remembers some awful thing that happened to him fifteen or twenty years ago, but the confusions and the panics of last year and the year before are too close for contentment."

His decision to confine his autobiography to a past so remote that he could no longer feel embarrassed by it should have been "seminal," too, but unfortunately has not been. Most autobiographers still insist on bringing their stories right up to the day they sat down at the word processor.

The consequences—books of stunning length and doubtful veracity—follow inevitably when the author discovers that while it is easy to write honestly about events of long ago, what happened last month is too painful to contemplate.

Thus we get outright fictions or a dense camouflage of irrelevant detail. Memoirs of Presidents and statesmen illustrate the vice at its worst.

They move along at a lively clip while covering the youthful years, only to bog down in tedium when they come to the great man's years of greatness.

The brevity Thurber achieved in "My Life and Hard Times" by stopping at 1918 seems almost inconceivable today when the typical biography feels more like a bludgeon than a book. Today the 400,000-word book is commonplace among biographers as well as historians, and it is no challenge for these people to go on for 500,000 or 600,000 words.

Part of the reason for this megatonnage is the proliferation of ghost writers and students hired to pile on detail until the reader slips to his knees sobbing for mercy. Then, too, with books now routinely priced at $20 to $30, perhaps people want more, even though more is almost always less when it's a five-pound book.

The electronic word processor connives in this literary bloat by making it child's play to turn out 500,000 words. Thurber wrote with a manual typewriter. A day's toil at one of those babies was hard labor. It took muscle to make the keys fly, and after every 10 or 12 words he had to reach forward and whip the heavy metal carriage back to the starting position before he could write another 10 words.

The Thurber House has a typewriter that might have been his, though Donn Vickers, the director, allows it might not. Having tried it, I am of the latter opinion, since the test suggested it would take about two weeks to write 800 words on it.

On the other hand, maybe that explains something. Thurber's pieces, all usually relatively short, are jewels of English writing. Maybe what America needs at this critical time, when everybody is bloating the language with dead ballast like "at this critical time," is more reading material that was written at the rate of 800 words per fortnight.

The preservation of The Thurber House suggests that despite talk about our galloping illiteracy Americans can still be hospitable to the written language when it is used with loving care.

"Now don't you dare drive all over town without gasoline!" Thurber's mother used to caution her sons when they got in the car. She said that in this very house with its rickety 1918 furniture and eyesore wallpaper, thus earning herself a place alongside Captain Ahab, Daisy Miller, Ma Joad and all those others who live on and on and on.

—RUSSELL BAKER

JAMES THURBER, 1894–1961

To summarize briefly James Thurber's life can be in some ways as precarious as explaining humor itself. The temptation to dwell on the preciosity of early 1900s Midwestern culture, or the quirkiness of his family members, or his own physical and mental difficulties can trivialize the work, which is, after all, what brings us to Thurber, one of the few canonical figures in American humor. Even though he was spared both military service and blacklisting by the House Un-American Activities Committee, his life and times may have been harder than many; still, his genius prevailed by twisting reality "to the right into humor rather than to the left into tragedy." Agonizing as it was for him, Thurber stands as the first modern American author whose reputation became that of a writer of short pieces.

I have provided factual landmarks, along with quotes from Thurber's autobiographical spoofs and partly fictive interviews, but as Thurber stated, pretending to write as his own biographer, "Thurber's life baffles and irritates the biographer because of its lack of design. One has the disturbing feeling that the man contrived to be some place without actually having gone there." Yet wherever it is he finally did manage to go, readers everywhere have been only too glad to follow.

"James Thurber was born in Columbus, Ohio, where so many awful things happened to him, on December 8, 1894. He was unable to keep anything on his stomach until he was seven years old but grew to be 6 feet 1¼ inches tall and to weigh a hundred fifty-four fully dressed for winter." He was "born in the blowy uplands of Columbus, Ohio, in a district know as 'the Flats,' which, for half of the year, was partially underwater and during the rest of the time was an outcropping of live granite, rising in dry weather to a height of two hundred feet. This condition led to moroseness, skepticism, jumping when shots were fired, membership in a silver cornet band, and, finally, a system of floating pulley-baskets by means of which the Thurber family was raised up to and lowered down from the second floor of the old family homestead."

In truth, Thurber's childhood included two significant and lifelong influences. The first was his mother's uncanny sense of dramatic humor, an eccentricity that may not have always made for an even-keeled family life but clearly inspired her son's comic interest and developed his ear for imitating speech. Moreover he inherited her extraordinary memory and stage presence. The second, a severe eye injury at age seven caused by an arrow during a game of William Tell, left him blind in one eye (eventually, "sympathetic opthalmia" overtook his other eye as an adult, leaving him totally blind). Owing to this, his school days began with a certain frailty and introspection. However, through the recognition of his writing and drawing abilities, his years at East High School blossomed with honors, including class presidency.

Thurber's studies at his hometown university, Ohio State, included formidable predicaments (which nonetheless became fodder for *My Life and Hard Times*) such as botany; instead of seeing "a vivid, restless clockwork of sharply defined plant cells," Thurber saw "what [looked] like a lot of milk." Another low point was mandatory military drill. "At 11 o'clock each morning thousands of freshmen and sophomores used to deploy over the campus, moodily creeping upon the old chemistry building. . . . As a soldier I was never any good at all. . . . Once General Littlefield, who was commandant of the cadet corps, popped up in front of me during regimental drill and snapped, 'You are the main trouble with this university!' I think he meant that my type was the main trouble with the university but he may have meant me individually."

Thurber did drop out of college temporarily during his sophomore year for his own program of reading and movie-going, but not before meeting Elliott Nugent, whose own theatrical gifts and energy redirected some of Thurber's unchanneled creativity. As a result of Nugent's influence, Thurber began to write for the school newspaper, edit the *Sundial*, OSU's humor magazine, and play active roles in The Strollers dramatic club, as a play- and songwriter. Without a degree, he left the university "in June, 1918, but I couldn't get into the army on account of my sight, just as grandfather couldn't get in on account of his age. He applied several times and each time he took off his coat and threatened to whip the men who said he was too old."

In *My Life and Hard Times*, which remained on bestseller lists for most of 1945, Thurber recounted the most memorable events of his college years living in and commuting by trolley from what is now The Thurber House, a literary center in the restored Victorian structure the Thurbers rented from 1913–1918. Since his father, Charles, worked for various public officials, in and out of jobs and favor as administrations changed, the family moved frequently.

"The mistaken exits and entrances of my thirties have moved me several times to some thought of spending the rest of my days wandering aimlessly around the South Seas, like a character out of Conrad, silent and inscrutable. But the necessity for frequent visits to my oculist and dentist has prevented this. . . . Nobody from Columbus has ever made a first-rate wanderer in the Conradean tradition. Some of them have been fairly good at disappearing for a few days to turn up in a hotel in Louisville with a bad headache and no recollection of how they got there." Though Thurber eventually resided in New York, Connecticut, Bermuda, and France, Columbus remained the wellspring for much of his best work. "In the early years of the nineteenth century, Columbus won out, as state capital, by one vote over Lancaster, and ever since then has had the hallucination that it is being followed, a curious municipal state of mind which affects, in some way or other, all those who live there. Columbus is a town in which almost anything is likely to happen and in which almost everything has."

In 1927, after a few years of reporting at the *Columbus Dispatch* (eventually earning his own first column, "Credos and Curios," a mixture of commentary, parody, cultural observations, and humor) Thurber tried a stint in France working at the Paris and then the Riviera edition of the *Tribune*. Married by then to Althea Adams, he weathered a series of frustrating attempts to sell some of his humorous pieces, and returned to the states to find a publisher. He had a book-length parody of current best-sellers, *Why We Behave Like Microbe Hunters,* which he ultimately abandoned.

As chance would have it, during that fruitless search he met E. B. White, who arranged a meeting for Thurber with Harold Ross, the editor of a struggling new magazine, *The New Yorker*. Thurber was hired as managing editor and, as he claimed, worked his way down to writer. In 1929, in collaboration with White, he published his first book, *Is Sex Necessary?* a parody of the popular sex and psychology books of the day. They wrote alternate chapters and Thurber provided quick pencil sketches that White inked. "It was, to be sure, E. B. White . . . who first began to look at my drawings critically. Like the discovery of San Salvador and the discovery of *pommes soufflés*, the discovery of my art was an accident."

With White's encouragement, Thurber began to submit drawings to *The New Yorker,* where he would publish hundreds of cartoons and spot illustrations before blindness overtook him. Dorothy Parker wrote in a preface to his collection of drawings, *The Seal in the Bedroom*, "These are strange people that Mr. Thurber has turned loose upon us. They seem to fall into three classes—the playful, the defeated, and the ferocious. All of them have the outer semblance of unbaked cookies. . . . It is curious, perhaps terrible, how Mr. Thurber has influenced the American face and physique, and some day he will surely answer for it. People didn't go about looking like that before he started drawing." Nor did cartoons themselves "go about looking like that" until Thurber arrived on the scene.

Thurber's drawings and spot illustrations graced the pages of *The New Yorker*—rarely working in color, he created very few covers—from 1930 (the first drawings were his "Pet Department") until 1947. For a bit longer, perpetuating Thurber's distinctive contributions, the magazine flipped previously drawn illustrations and had Thurber write new captions.

Thurber artwork, at its peak, also powered advertising campaigns for Fisher Body, Bug-a-Boo insecticide, and the French Line cruise ships; companies such as Bergdorf Goodman manufactured ties, dresses, and tableware with Thurber's figures; art directors engaged Thurber to create book covers as well as folios of interior illustrations for a dog care manual, a book of curious etymologies, and even a book on fashion titled *Men Can Take It*. On the arrival of Thurber's 1943 collection of drawings, *Men, Women and Dogs,* the popular British fiction writer W. Somerset Maugham wrote, "It's the perfect book to turn over while one is drinking a cocktail. The only thing against it is that it makes a cocktail seem rather wan and pale." Accolades from British art critic Paul Nash and painter George Grosz made Thurber particularly proud, as did a response reported to him from Henri Matisse: "a man named Thurber . . . is the only good artist you have in New York."

He was profligate with his drawings, giving them away at parties, and often told interviewers that if you stretched out all the drawings, they would create "a mile and half of lines." As his eyesight failed, he attempted to create pictures using white chalk on black paper, which the printer would then reverse. He used a Zeiss loop around his head, much as a jeweler might, to magnify his work (calling himself a welder from Mars) until his sight failed completely in 1951, after a series of painful, stressful operations.

Thurber divorced Althea after twelve difficult years, and married Helen Wismer, about whom biographer Harrison Kinney writes, "Of the twenty-six years they were married, Thurber was legally blind through twenty-one of them, and that he kept going as long and as well as he did may be credited in large part to Helen's care." She was his business manager, companion, editor, helpmate, "seeing-eye wife," and nurse. Between 1930 and 1961, Thurber published nearly thirty books. Many of them collected the unparalleled breadth of pieces written for *The New Yorker* and other magazines: the "casuals" and "Talk of the Town" contributions; profiles of tennis stars and nearly forgotten public figures; parodies of his contemporaries, pulp magazines, and current events; and scores of stories such as "The Catbird Seat," and "The Secret Life of Walter Mitty," two of the most anthologized pieces of modern fiction. Thurber widely contributed articles on subjects ranging from the international spy situation to the future of photography, from the development of the bicycle to Byrd's discoveries in Antarctica. Though he could hardly claim genuine familiarity with these topics, he addressed each with the borrowed tone and speech of an expert, therein creating a style of humor that has outlasted generations of imitators.

Thurber also published five children's books; two collections of fables; *The Last Flower,* a parable in pictures, which was E. B. White's favorite of all Thurber's books; *The Male Animal*, a play co-authored with Elliott Nugent, which was a

Broadway hit in 1940 and again in 1952; and three volumes of memoirs. *My Life and Hard Times* was published in 1933. *A Thurber Album*, a later reconsidering of the family, friends, and mentors from his Columbus years, appeared in 1952. Finally, in 1959, two years before his death, the enormously successful *The Years with Ross* appeared serially in the *Atlantic Monthly* and then as a book, conjuring a portrait of *The New Yorker* magazine and its founding editor; in some critics' minds, the work might have been equally alternately titled *The Years with Thurber*.

Encroaching blindness plagued his last decade, as well as what he considered the short-sightedness of *The New Yorker*'s changing attitudes and staff. Partly because his memory held so many options for him, much of Thurber's later work revels in wordplay, interior monologues, and restless manipulations of language. His essays often veered toward diatribes, as his attention preoccupied itself with the harassing climate of McCarthyism, the blight of America's slovenliness with locution, the ill-preparedness of youth, and the darkening or even dearth of humor—or so he perceived it.

Thurber continued to write up until his death, prevailing upon his photographic memory not only for content but for containment as well. He had known of his extraordinary powers of retention since adolescence and was confirmed in them by a college psychology test, and Thurber began to compose nearly two thousand words of prose—only a bit shorter than the length of this biographical note—sharpening and shaping the language for hours, until a secretary or his wife Helen came for dictation, as if merely printing the negatives that Thurber had taken in his mind. Among his unpublished papers are many drafts of novels and plays that, despite continual rewriting, he could not resolve. One wonders what eyesight might have enabled him to complete.

The burdens of his physical and mental condition gradually overtook him. Thurber continued to be a vivacious raconteur, a passionate debater, and, often enough, an exasperating dinner guest. Thurber once described himself in print, and, perhaps, in jest: "He never listens when anybody else is talking, preferring to keep his mind a blank until they get through so he can talk." Finally, the diagnosis of a toxic-thyroid condition explained some of the erratic behavior, though his lifelong bouts with and abstinence from alcohol often exasperated problems. As his friend, the novelist Peter De Vries wrote, "If in his art he told the truth, in his life he told it off." Or, as Thurber confessed to *Life* magazine in 1960, "I am in a corner without being back there and often come out fighting."

Shortly before his death, Thurber did enjoy the publication of his last book, *Lanterns and Lances*, and another Broadway success, the Tony Award–winning *A Thurber Carnival*, a theatrical revue of his work directed by Burgess Meredith.

Thurber collapsed one evening after a theater opening of Noel Coward's latest play. He was rushed to a hospital in New York City, where a tumor was removed from his brain. He endured a month there in a coma before succumbing on November 2, 1961. His remains were sent to Columbus, Ohio, for burial in Greenlawn Cemetery.

Posthumously, several additional volumes were published. Helen Thurber prepared *Thurber & Co.* and *Credos and Curios* and, with Edward Weeks, edited a volume of *Selected Letters*. In 1989, I undertook the editing of uncollected writings and drawings, subsequently published as *Collecting Himself: James Thurber on Writing and Writers, Humor and Himself*. In 1994, I edited another compilation of uncollected work for the centennial of Thurber's birth, *People Have More Fun Than Anybody*. Subsequently a consummate biography of Thurber appeared, written by Harrison Kinney who had begun the work as a graduate project during Thurber's tenure at *The New Yorker*, and the Library of America published an authoritative one-volume anthology of Thurber's work, further establishing

James Thurber as the preeminent American humorist of the century.

E. B. White's obituary in *The New Yorker* included the following passage: "His mind was never at rest, and his pencil was connected to his mind by the best conductive tissue I have ever seen in action. . . . you had to sit next to him day after day to understand the extravagance of his clowning, the wildness and subtlety of his thinking, and the intensity of his interest in others and his sympathy for their dilemmas—dilemmas that he constantly enlarged, put in focus, and made immortal." Journalist Henry Brandon suggested that Thurber's secret was "a warm heart and an angry mind." Perhaps this can serve as a definition of the literary humorist, as least as Thurber has identified it, and a reason why so many readers the world over have needed such a figure to correct our vision of the world and the sometimes failed, glorious, eccentric, noble, and puny lives we live within it.

—MICHAEL J. ROSEN, literary director of The Thurber House, the literary center in James Thurber's restored boyhood home, has edited collections of Thurber's work and is currently editor of *Mirth of a Nation: The Best Contemporary Humor*.

MY LIFE
AND
HARD TIMES

✒

1933

Written in the midst of a great economic depression, the ironically
titled *My Life and Hard Times* confines its attention to a world
of Midwestern culture, school days, and family life—an idio-
syncratic world above and beyond the genuine problems of a
nation.

Thurber much admired Clarence Day—they both drew,
they both found animals a distinctive means of revealing
human character, they both published in *The New Yorker*—and
Day's short memoirs of his own family had just begun to
appear in magazines (and later collected in his books such as
Life with Father). These emboldened Thurber to embrace the
eccentricities of his own family in his first attempt at autobiog-
raphy-inspired stories. For years, Thurber, an effervescent
raconteur, had been rehearsing bits of these stories at dinner
parties, honing recollection into the even more memorable
guise of fiction. As Thurber's first biographer, Charles Holmes,
writes, those comedic figures of his youth—assorted maids,
illiterate ball players, elders stuck in Civil War visions, frail
aunts—"represent freedom, independence, the irrepressible
stuff of life which refuses to be caught in formulas and conven-
tions."

In each story, Thurber took an illogical assumption or
wayward predicament, and naturalized it through his own

quirky logic. His sentences are so perfectly minted (and regularly held up as gems of clarity and composition) that the reader trusts the author, even though the irrational has assumed the character of the rational. The stories' escalating plots finally impose an odd calm amid the calamity, an assurance of a sort, as though caught up in the surprises of Thurber's far-fetched goings-on, the reader feels the sigh and pleasure of recognition. Adapting Wordworth's comment about poetry, he once defined humor as "emotional chaos told about calmly and quietly in retrospect." Clifton Fadiman commented of Thurber, "Great comic literature teaches us how to fail without really trying," and certainly *My Life and Hard Times* is Thurber's best effort at providing the releasing laughter of hindsight, the lifesaving relief of storytelling.

In a *New York Times* interview of 1940, Thurber claimed his writings were based on truth, but distorted. The need for humor to be taken seriously, and, moreover, to be seen as essentially serious at its heart, perennially concerned Thurber. He was especially proud of T. S. Eliot's fondness for this book because the poet understood its essential seriousness.

My Life and Hard Times, Thurber's fourth book, was preceded by *Is Sex Necessary?* (1929, co-authored with E. B. White), *The Owl in the Attic and Other Perplexities* (1931), and a collection of drawings, *The Seal in the Bedroom and Other Predicaments* (1932). Harper & Brothers printed a modest first edition of three thousand copies of *My Life* in November 1933, but over the next couple of years went back to press a dozen times.

An edition was released in the United Kingdom by Harper in 1934, and other editions continued: one from Penguin (U.K.), an "Armed Forces Edition," and another from Bantam. Both Blue Ribbon Books and Hamish Hamilton (U.K.) packaged the book with Thurber's earlier collection,

The Owl in the Attic. Foreign-language editions ensued, as well as constant requests to reprint individual stories in textbooks, readers, and anthologies.

Ernest Hemingway's clowning words graced the original cover; while partly intended to poke at Gertrude Stein with whom he'd suffered a falling out, his stature clearly conferred welcome upon a relatively unknown author: "I find it superior to the autobiography of Henry Adams. Even in the earliest days when Thurber was writing under the name Alice B. Toklas we knew he had it in him if he could get it out."

Frank Sullivan in the *New York Herald Tribune* wrote, "It is one of the most important and revealing human documents we have seen since Rousseau gave us his immortal *Confessions* (which I must read some time). Furthermore, Rousseau's *Confessions* suffered from the drawback of not being illustrated by Thurber, and to my way of thinking, this is a grave handicap for any book. For that matter, I'm not convinced that Rousseau's *Confessions* did not suffer from the handicap of not being *written* by Thurber."

The stories of this book have become American classics. There are few stories more anthologized, read aloud, and laughed over. If the internet had been operational in 1933, the popularity of these stories would have ensured their email voyage into every home. Even people who have never read an entire book of Thurber's, know the ghost that got in, the bed that fell, and the day the dam supposedly broke. Entire generations of writers cite Thurber as a model and early influence: John Updike, Garrison Keillor, Tony Kushner, Edward Albee, and Spalding Gray, just to note a few.

The financial success of *My Life and Hard Times,* and its sale to Hollywood (a little known film, *Rise and Shine*, starring Jack Oakie as the football player Bolenciecwcz from "University Days"), allowed Thurber to give up full-time work at *The New Yorker*. He remained on staff, contributing his own cartoons, casuals, and short stories, and also editing and rewriting others' "Talk of the Town" pieces. *My Life and Hard Times* provided Thurber with the confirmation of his status as an important writer, and the confidence he needed to prevail over the even harder times ahead.

—M. J. R.